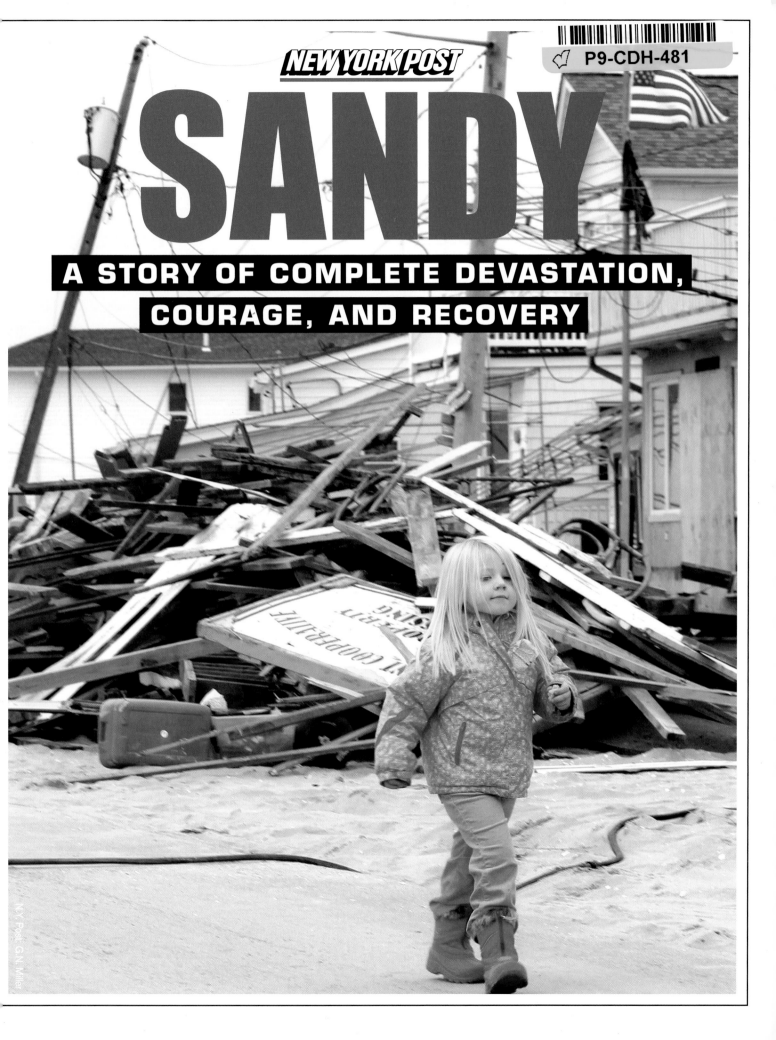

NEW YORK POST

SANDY

A STORY OF COMPLETE DEVASTATION, COURAGE, AND RECOVERY

NY Post: G.N. Miller

Two weeks after Sandy hit the New York region, sand piles and damaged vehicles remained on Ocean Avenue in Brooklyn. (N.Y. Post: Charles Wenzelberg)

This book is available in quantity at special discounts for your group or organization.
For further information, contact:

Triumph Books LLC
814 North Franklin Street
Chicago, Illinois 60610
Phone: (312) 337-0747
www.triumphbooks.com

Printed in U.S.A.
ISBN: 978-1-60078-918-2

Content packaged by Mojo Media, Inc.
Joe Funk: Editor
Jason Hinman: Creative Director

Front and back cover photos by New York Post: Chad Rachman.

CONTENTS

INTRODUCTION

By Andy Soltis

It was huge, powerful and terrifying, so much so that forecasters gave it names like "Frankenstorm" more than a week before it touched U.S. land. Hurricane Sandy would wreak havoc in more than a dozen states, killing nearly 300 people in seven countries, creating wind gusts as far west as Wisconsin and as far north as Canada, causing water levels to rise from Florida to Maine and inflicting Katrina-level damage.

But she saved her worst for the Northeast, including New York, New Jersey and the region.

We'd never seen anything like Sandy, which destroyed whole neighborhoods, turning parts of Brooklyn, Queens, Staten Island and Hoboken into ghost towns. Miles and miles of the famed Jersey Shore were sunk under tons of water as the tide rose to at least eight feet above normal. Large swaths of Long Island, Westchester and Connecticut were without power for weeks — just a year after taking a hit from Hurricane Irene. Lower Manhattan was dark for five days and hospitals near the surging East River had to scramble to evacuate bed-ridden patients.

The misery was everywhere, the personal tragedies unending.

A Staten Island mother tried to lead her sons, 2 and 4, to safety the night Sandy arrived but the raging storm ripped them from her arms. Their bodies were finally found in marshland, three days later, by cops in wet suits.

A 29-year-old Flushing, Queens man was killed in his bedroom when a tree branch at least three feet wide fell into his home.

The body of a 66-year-old former Marine, who lived alone with his cat, was only discovered in his flooded Staten Island home after 11 days.

There were also stories of heroism and sacrifice. A man walking his dog on deserted downtown Hubert Street when Sandy made landfall found himself in chest-high water and certain he would drown. But alert security officers pulled him — and his dog — to safety.

Photographs told their own stunning stories. They showed war-zone-like debris where 111 homes once stood in Breezy Point. An entire fleet of taxi cabs under water in a Hoboken parking lot. The red-and-yellow marquis sign of the 87-year-old Shore Theater in Staten Island crumpled like building blocks.

A giant tanker ship sitting strangely ashore along Front Street on Staten Island. A Bay Head, N.J. man digging though mounds and mounds of sand in his living room. And the entire facade of a four-story apartment building in the Chelsea section of Manhattan ripped away, leaving it like a see-through dollhouse.

Quickly the enormity of the damage sunk in. Forty-eight deaths were reported in the New York area. Nearly 8,000 trees had fallen in the city. More than two million people in New York State and

As Sandy hit, free sand bags were made available in Brooklyn's Red Hook neighborhood. (N.Y. Post: Spencer Burnett)

Forty-eight deaths were reported in the New York area. Nearly 8,000 trees had fallen in the city. More than two million people in New York State and another 2.5 million in New Jersey were without power. Lost business counted in the tens of billions of dollars — and many companies never reopened.

another 2.5 million in New Jersey were without power. Lost business counted in the tens of billions of dollars — and many companies never reopened.

But the region fought to come back, buoyed by President Obama, who consoled the suddenly homeless and hopeless in New Jersey two days after the storm, followed by a visit to Staten Island two weeks later. Marines pitched in with emergency workers at the Midland Beach section of Staten Island.

New York's public schools reopened after a week. A tottering building crane, which broke loose high above W. 57th Street and forced the evacuation of neighboring buildings, was secured and residents were allowed back into their buildings after six days. Parks, libraries and city offices slowly got back to normal. The New York Knicks-Brooklyn Nets opening game was delayed but the New York Giants game the Sunday after Sandy was played on schedule at MetLife Stadium.

Still, there were new problems that didn't go away. Enormous lines at gasless gas stations and power outages that lasted in some neighborhoods for weeks. Officials estimated the damage would cost upward of $75 billion and take the region more than a year to recover.

The badly bruised spirit of the region consoled itself with the generous efforts of many who pitched in.

Bruce Springsteen, Jon Bon Jovi, Eric Clapton and a host of others performed at a Madison Square Garden concert to benefit Sandy victims. Newlyweds Justin Timberlake and Jessica Biel passed out relief supplies in the Rockaways.

And it wasn't all big names who helped.

A Brooklyn man spearheaded a toy drive and traded his business suit for a Santa costume so he could bring a little Christmas to kids in battered Belle Harbor.

A Secret Sandy charity was formed and quickly got 3,200 donors to provide Christmas gifts to 1,800 families in need.

Even families that lost loved ones in the 2001 crash of Flight 587 in the Rockaways took up a collection for residents of the devastated neighborhood.

They remembered what pain felt like. And what courage looked like. So would anyone who lived through Sandy. ■

An aerial view captures the devastation along the coast in Rockaway Beach, Queens. (N.Y. Post: Matthew McDermott)

Part 1

BRINGING
HELL AND
HIGH WATER

A massive tanker named the John B. Caddell, built in 1941, washed ashore on Staten Island during Hurricane Sandy. The Manhattan skyline can be seen in the background beyond the ship, which weighed more than 700 tons. (N.Y. Post: Chad Rachman)

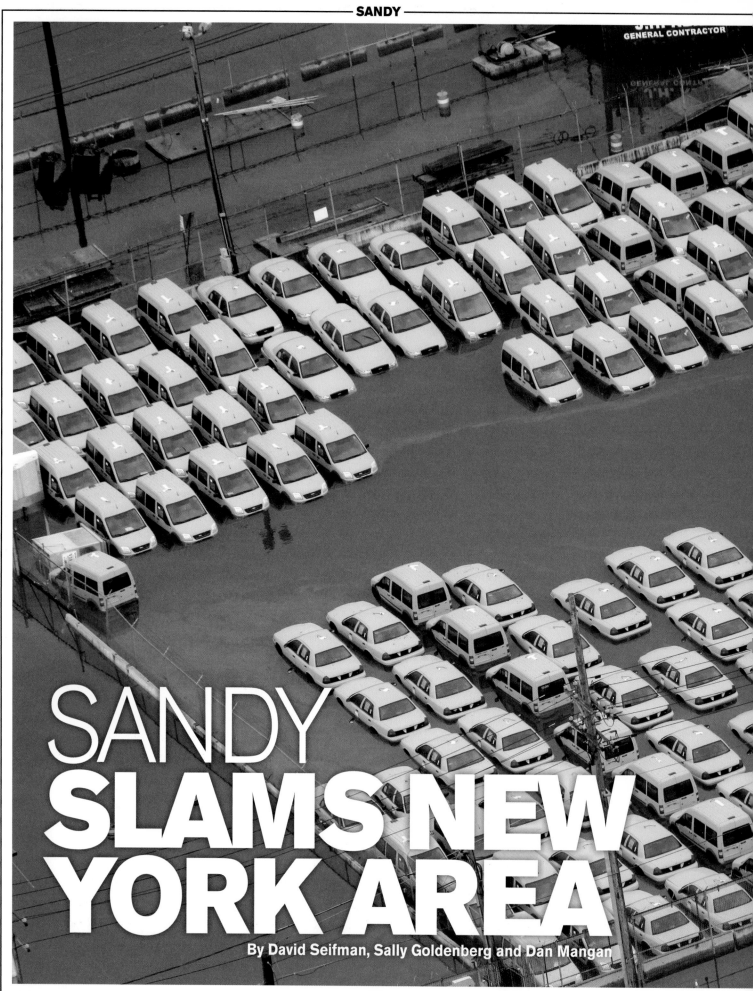

SANDY SLAMS NEW YORK AREA

By David Seifman, Sally Goldenberg and Dan Mangan

Mass Floods, Outages Wreak Havoc

Hurricane Sandy blasted the New York area on Monday, October 29, 2012. The storm, its winds flirting with 100 mph, unleashed a wave of devastation from which it could take weeks to recover.

In flooded lower Manhattan, water gushed into the Brooklyn Battery Tunnel and cars were floating in the streets.

There was no dry land anywhere in the Rockaways, where cops in the 100th Precinct station house were trapped on the building's second floor.

As Sandy reached land near Atlantic City, it was downgraded to a tropical storm after its winds weakened slightly.

The punishing storm:

- Killed a 29-year-old man in his Flushing, Queens, home when a tree fell into the building. The victim, Tony Laino, was found in his bedroom by three neighbors who went to rescue him. The branch that fell on him was at least three feet wide. Witnesses said the victim's devastated dad was crying out for his son. The family has lived there for more than 20 years.

- Claimed the lives of three children, at least two whom were killed when a tree fell in North Salem.

- Caused the death of woman, who was electrocuted after stepping into a puddle on 105th Avenue in South Richmond Hill.

- Left NYU Langone Medical Center dark after back-up generators failed. Patients had to be moved to other facilities.

- Generated a storm surge worsened by a higher full-moon tide, with the peak of the flooding engulfing lower Manhattan and other low-lying areas at 8 p.m.

Call 'em yellow submarines. This fleet of taxis would be better off as a fleet of ships as they sit with engines – and everything else – flooded in a Weehawken, New Jersey, parking lot. The New Jersey city suffered devastating storm damage as a result of Hurricane Sandy's destructive surge. (AP Images)

- Forced the MTA to continue its crippling closure of all trains, buses and subways until at least tomorrow. All flights have been canceled from area airports, and the flood-prone Brooklyn Battery and Holland tunnels were shut down indefinitely.

- Knocked out power to at least 448,000 city customers by last night — 250,000 in Manhattan. Most were below 39th Street.

- Left more than half of Long Islanders without power as 650,000 people had outages as of 8 p.m. last night.

- Led to forced evacuations for up to 375,000 people from low-lying areas in New York's Zone A — although some refused to leave their homes. More than 3,000 people were in city emergency shelters by midday.

Gov. Cuomo deployed about 2,000 National Guard troops to deal with Hurricane Sandy's fury.

He warned there may be prolonged power outages because Sandy was affecting "potentially the entire Eastern Seaboard" — meaning fewer crews will be able to leave their home states to help New York.

Sandy's storm surge could break the record of 10½ feet set by Hurricane Donna in 1960, said state Operations Director Howard Glaser. Tropical Storm Irene in 2011 had a 4-foot storm surge that rose to a maximum of 9½ feet.

On Coney Island, Chmi Gaiger stood marveling at the roiling, white-capped Atlantic before Sandy's full force was felt.

Gaiger, 42, said he was there "to see something you have never seen before and that you'll never see in your lifetime again. To see the big power."

Harried cops used sirens and horns to warn about a dozen storm watchers off the end of a Coney Island pier near Stillwell Avenue.

"Get out of here!" the cops yelled.

Philip Ellis, 53, of Flatbush, did more than just watch — he went for his daily swim, and lived to tell the tale.

"It was just way too turbulent, too much of a riptide. I couldn't stay in more than 10 minutes," said the former airline employee, who emerged purple-lipped and shivering from the surf.

Sandy's storm surge hits a small tree in Bridgeport, Connecticut's Seaside Park on Oct. 29. Water from the Long Island Sound spilled into roadways and towns along the Connecticut shoreline. (AP Images)

"You don't get much of a chance to experience what it's like to swim right before a hurricane. It was exciting, exhilarating."

More fearful of Sandy was Steve Geykhman, 25, a marking manager who lives on Surf Avenue in nearby Sea Gate.

"I got the whole house boarded up," Geykhman said. "I'm expecting the worst.

"My whole family left, and I'm protecting the fort. I have my whole survival kit ready: water, dry cereal, some cigarettes, flashlights, candles."

On Staten Island, South Side Hardware Co. owner James Rachmiel said, "We are sold out of mostly everything.

"People have been buying tarps, hoses, batteries. People are panic buying," Rachmiel said. "I think people are taking it more seriously than last year."

Great Kills resident Alex Rubin, 44, an environmental engineer, was among those stocking up, saying, "I'm leaving now. The water is coming up the block.

"I'm used to flooding, but it's going to be bad... My wife is worried — that's why we're leaving." ■

Additional reporting by Julia Marsh, Antonio Antenucci, Larry Celona, Lorena Mongelli, Kate Kowsh, Philip Messing Kenneth Garger and Kieran Crowley

Left: Murray Street in TriBeCa near St. John's University's Manhattan campus flooded during Sandy, leaving vehicles nearly submerged. (N.Y. Post: William C. Lopez) Above: Sandy's destruction hit the Mansion Marina in Staten Island's Great Kills neighborhood, tossing boats and leaving dozens of vessels on land. (N.Y. Post: Chad Rachman)

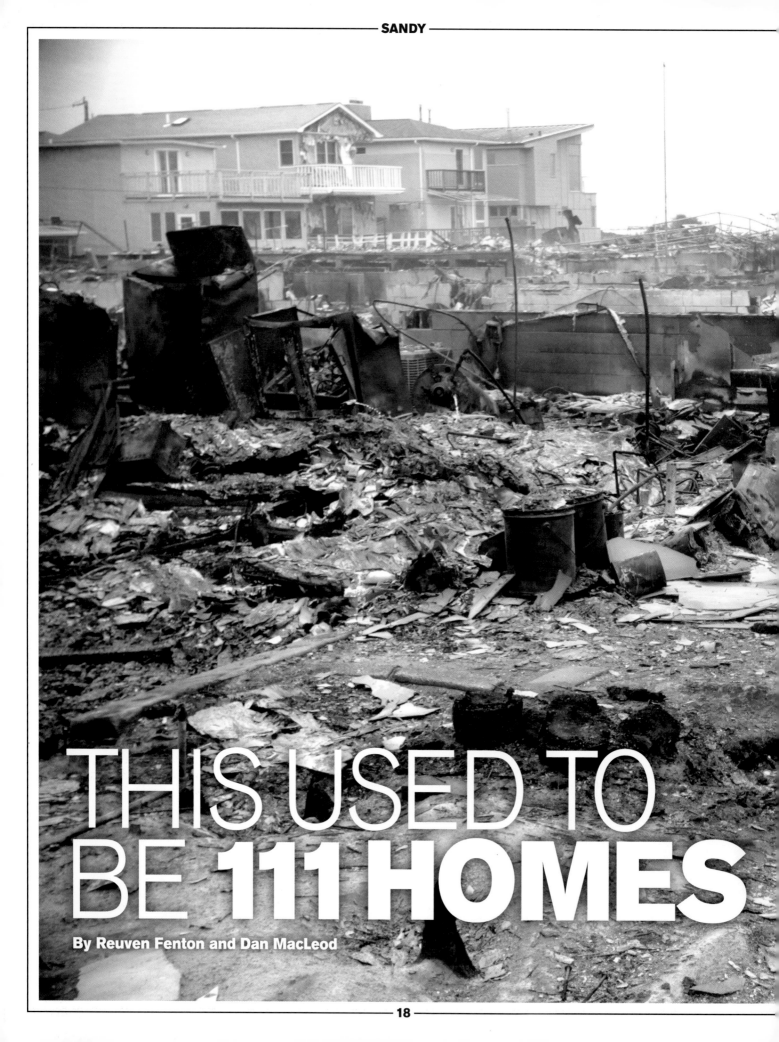

THIS USED TO BE 111 HOMES

By Reuven Fenton and Dan MacLeod

Fire Devastates Beachfront Community in Breezy Point, Queens

The idyllic beachfront community of Breezy Point, Queens, was laid bare by a devastating fire — fueled by Hurricane Sandy's 70-mph winds — that destroyed 111 houses and damaged another 20 as surging floodwaters initially kept firefighters at bay.

Emergency crews had to contend with the flooding, wind and low fire-hydrant pressure for nearly 12 hours to douse the horrifying six-alarm blaze, which kicked up around 11 p.m. on Monday, October 29.

It may have initially started as an electrical fire that quickly jumped from house to house, officials said.

Thomas and Missy Rom and their four kids, among the handful of residents who defied evacuation orders, narrowly escaped.

"We saw the water rising and said, 'We can fight water.' But when the fire came, we knew we couldn't fight," said Thomas. "We saw houses on fire, and the fire was jumping from one house to the next. That's when we left."

Thomas pushed his son on a surfboard to flee to a neighbor's house. Then they had to escape as the flames spread to that home.

Tuesday, the Roms dug through the rubble that used to be their home.

"We just wanted to see if there's anything left," Thomas said. "There isn't — it's just memories now. I built this house 20 years ago and now I saw the end of it."

Ashes and rubble mark the area where 111 homes were destroyed by fast-spreading fires in Breezy Point, Queens, while flooding kept firefighters away. It took 12 hours to fight the blaze, which began on Oct. 29. (N.Y. Post: William C. Lopez)

Taken by storm

Hurricane Sandy stormed into the tri-state area Oct. 29, packing sustained winds of 90 mph and gusts up to 110 mph before slamming into New Jersey.

2 p.m. Thurs.
2 p.m. Fri.
2 p.m. Weds.
2 p.m. Tues.

NH
MA
NY
CT
PA
NJ
OH

Projected track of the storm

2 p.m. Nov. 1

*As of 8 p.m.

2 p.m. Oct. 31

2 p.m. Oct. 30

2 p.m. Oct. 29

LONG ISLAND

Long Beach
Winds: 45- 47 mph, gusts 73 mph
Rain: 0.5 inches
Flooding: Breaking waves of 15 to 20 feet
Impact: 8,000 power outages; mandatory evacuation area
Islip
Winds: 41-44 mph, gusts 90 mph
Rain: 0.7 inches
Flooding: Flooded roads
Impact: Epicenter of power loss on Long Island; evacuations along coast and in trailer parks
Bayville
Winds: 45 mph, gusts 85 mph
Rain: 0.45 inches
Flooding: Waves of 15 to 20 feet breaking on roadway
Impact: Two roads connecting Bayville to main island washed out
Westhampton
Winds: 45-47 mph, gusts 59 mph
Rain: 0.48 inches
Flooding: Village Marina flooded
Impact: Evacuations along coast

CONNECTICUT

Stamford/Greenwich
Winds: 40 mph, gusts 76 mph
Rain: 0.32 inches
Flooding: Roads flooded
Impact: 26,000 power outages; three firehouses evacuated
Fairfield
Winds: 39-41 mph, gusts 76 mph
Rain: 0.32 inches
Flooding: Roads flooded
Impact: Evacuations along coast

WESTCHESTER

White Plains
Winds: 34-37 mph, gusts 59 mph
Rain: 0.45 inches
Flooding: Roads flooded
Impact: Hundreds of power outages

NEW YORK CITY

MANHATTAN
Central Park
Winds: 35-45 mph, gusts 62 mph
Rain: 0.52 inches
Flooding: N/A
Impact: Snapped and fallen tree branches
Financial District/Battery Park City
Winds: 35-45 mph, gusts 65 mph
Rain: 0.55 inches
Flooding: Surge of 12.5 feet
Impact: Seawall breached at Battery, a mandatory evacuation area. Con Ed shuts off power.
BROOKLYN
Coney Island-Sea Gate
Winds: 45 to 50 mph, gusts up to 70 mph
Rain: 0.5 inches
Flooding: Surge of 11 feet
Impact: 3,600 power outages; mandatory evacuation
Bay Ridge
Winds: 45 to 50 mph, gusts up to 70 mph
Rain: 0.5 inches
Flooding: Surge of 8 feet
Impact: Numerous downed trees
QUEENS
Rockaways
Winds: 45 mph, gusts up to 72 mph
Rain: 0.5 inches
Flooding: Surge of 11 feet, breaking waves of 15 to 20 feet. Streets 3 feet underwater

Impact: Mandatory evacuation area
STATEN ISLAND
New Dorp Beach
Winds: 45 to 50 mph, gusts up to 70 mph
Rain: 0.5 inches
Flooding: Reports of flooded streets, surge of 10 feet
Impact: Sporadic power outages
BRONX
Throggs Neck, Bronx
Winds: 40 mph, gusts up to 68 mph
Rain: 0.5 inches
Flooding: Reports of flooded streets, surge of 12.1 feet
Impact: Seawall breached

NEW JERSEY

Atlantic City
Winds: 55-60 mph, gusts 64 mph
Rain: 5.1 inches
Flooding: 8.3 feet (broke record from 1985's Hurricane Gloria)
Impact: 30,000 evacuated; portions of Garden State Parkway closed
Seaside Heights
Winds: 50-55 mph, gusts 73 mph
Rain: 2.5 inches
Flooding: Flooding reported on boardwalk and inland streets
Impact: Mandatory evacuation
Jersey City
Winds: 40 mph, gusts 70 mph
Rain: 0.49 inches
Impact: First floor and basement apartments evacuated

Track of Hurricane Sandy

Sources: Accuweather, National Weather Service, state and local agencies

NY Post graphic: Ana Gioia

A helicopter view shows the beachfront community of Breezy Point, Queens, following a six-alarm fire that kicked up late at night on Oct. 29. The blaze destroyed 111 homes and damaged another 20 as surging floodwaters blocked the path of area firefighters. (N.Y. Post: Matthew McDermott)

Tom Hammill, 60, lived on Fulton Walk with his wife and two daughters. Now all that remains of his house is the back porch.

"I came here to say goodbye. I could see from afar that nothing was left standing. This is total devastation," he said Tuesday.

The storm surge made it impossible for firefighters to immediately get to the isolated neighborhood at the tip of the Rockaway Peninsula. The flames broke out around high tide, when streets were filled with five feet of water.

"Our trucks were initially unable to move due to the flooding. When the water stared to recede, we started working in the area," said Marty Ingram, chief of Breezy Point's Volunteer Fire Department, which works with the FDNY.

"With the wind, it was like a blowtorch last night. It happened at the peak of the tide. We couldn't move in. It destroyed five blocks."

At one point, more than 30 cops who normally would have responded, were stranded inside the 100th Precinct station house by floodwaters, and could not escape using the city-provided rowboats due to a strong current.

"It was no different from when you saw the pictures on TV of [Hurricane] Katrina — the streets just became rivers," said one law-enforcement source.

And Mayor Bloomberg said that motorboats could not be used.

"We had plenty of motor boats; they just can't go where the water isn't very deep," said Bloomberg.

Nearly 200 firefighters battled the blaze, and some residents had to be rescued by boat.

Miraculously, FDNY Commissioner Sal Cassano reported, there were no serious injuries or reports of missing people.

"The worst thing I saw like this was the Trade Center. I never saw anything like this in 34 years on the job. This looks like Berlin in WWII," said FDNY Deputy Assistant Chief Jack Mooney.

"The city was just strapped. It was an impossible night." ■

Additional reporting by Larry Celona, Jessica Simeone and Sally Goldenberg

DROWNTOWN
NEW JERSEY

By Jeane MacIntosh

Utter Havoc Throughout State

Superstorm Sandy ripped through New Jersey on Monday, October 29, and Tuesday, October 30, leaving entire towns underwater, boardwalks demolished, 2.5 million households without power and at least five dead in an unprecedented trail of destruction.

Gov. Chris Christie said the winds and sea surges left "absolute devastation" as train stations flooded, fallen trees blocked streets, railroad cars washed onto the Turnpike, boardwalk rides crashed into the ocean, and homes came off their foundations and floated down roadways.

"There are no words to describe what's been New Jersey's experience over the last 24 hours, and what we'll have to contend with over the coming days, weeks and months," he said.

"The level of devastation is beyond anything I ever thought I'd see," Christie said. "It's unthinkable."

After speaking with Christie, President Obama expedited the state's designation as major disaster area, with eight counties getting immediate emergency aid.

Two-thirds of the state, or 2.5 million customers, remained without power, double the number during Hurricane Irene. About 460,000 of those outages were caused by the surge that flooded substations along the Passaic, Hackensack and Raritan rivers.

The National Guard was deployed, and search-and-rescue crews combed for stranded residents in Atlantic City and the Jersey Shore towns of Seaside Park, Lavallette and Ortley Beach, which Christie said were "nearly completely underwater."

The Jersey Shore borough of Tuckerton was nearly swallowed up by the storm-swollen Atlantic on Oct. 30. (AP Images)

Jersey Shore's Ride to Ruin

A wrecked roller coaster that once sat on the Funtown Pier — and came to rest in the Atlantic Ocean — was a grim symbol of Hurricane Sandy's wrath as stunned Jersey Shore residents got their first chance to see the horrific damage in the days following the storm.

The roller coaster was a star attraction of Seaside Heights until Sandy came ashore, when a section of the pier collapsed and was washed up on the beach.

Homeowners returned to Point Pleasant Beach for the first time since Sandy and found a wet wasteland.

"A lot of tears are being shed," said Dennis Cucci, whose home sustained heavy damage. "It's absolutely mindboggling."

"It looks like a bomb went off here," said Barbara Montemarano after she and husband Robert drove to see what was left of their condo near the ocean.

"There's almost nobody here; it looks like tumbleweeds are rolling down the street."

About half of Point Pleasant Beach's famous mile-long boardwalk was either destroyed or seriously damaged by the storm — yet a large central section of the boardwalk survived unscathed.

—**Kate Kowsh**

Part of Atlantic City's iconic boardwalk washed into the streets, while the roller coaster from Seaside Heights' amusement park wound up in the Atlantic.

Farther north in Bergen County, crews and good Samaritans used canoes, power boats and even Jet Skis to evacuate residents in Little Falls and Moonachie after the Hackensack River flowed over a natural berm.

"Around 10 p.m. [Monday], water just started rushing down the street...There was no stopping it," Little Ferry resident Stefania Davi told NBC News.

More than 400 people were evacuated to shelters.

"Monday night, this block was like a big lake," longtime Hoboken resident Joseph Marra, 80, said as he waited for a pump to help clear his home of waist-deep water.

"This happened in 20 minutes. All of a sudden, it was shooting in from the yard like there was a pump out there," he said.

Entire sections of NJ Transit's North Jersey Coast Line and the Kearny Junction were washed out in what transit officials called "unprecedented" damage. ■

Additional reporting by Kate Kowsh and Post Wire Services

Left: An iconic roller coaster that had been part of the SeaView Heights boardwalk for more than 70 years sits in the Atlantic Ocean. Above: Governor Chris Christie describes the damage to the Jersey Shore during an Oct. 30 press conference. (AP Images)

SANDY'S TOLL IN NEW YORK STATE

Estimate of Sandy's cost:	$41.9B	Housing damaged or destroyed:	305,000	Power outages	2.19M	Businesses impacted	265,300

Housing damaged or destroyed in Louisiana during Katrina: 214,700
Power outages: 800,000 • Businesses impacted: 18,700

TOPPED
KATRINA

Sandy's Price Tag Estimated at $42 Billion

By Carl Campanile, Jennifer Fermino and David Seifman

On November 26, Gov. Cuomo put the first official price tag on the economic damage inflicted on the state by Hurricane Sandy — a staggering $42 billion, with $19 billion in the city alone.

He argued that the devastation wreaked by the storm statewide was worse than what Hurricane Katrina did to Louisiana in 2005.

"Hurricane Katrina, in many ways, was not as impactful as Hurricane Sandy, believe it or not," Cuomo said. "Because of the density of New York, the number of people affected, the number of properties affected was much larger in Hurricane Sandy than Hurricane Katrina. This puts the entire conversation, I believe, into focus...Now Katrina had a human toll that thankfully we have not paid in this region."

Katrina and its subsequent floods claimed 1,866 lives, compared with the more than 100 taken by Sandy.

Figures released by Cuomo's office showed 305,000 homes were damaged or destroyed by Sandy, compared with 214,700 for Katrina in Louisiana. The number of businesses hit here was put at 265,300, against 18,700 in Louisiana. There were 2.19 million power outages here, 800,000 during Katrina.

Cuomo put a $41.9 billion price tag on Sandy's hit to the state, which included both the city's costs and $9.1 billion in what was described as "mitigation and prevention" of future storms.

Repairs to the subways and commuter rail lines alone were expected to cost about $5 billion.

Katrina's hit on Louisiana was $80 billion.

Both Cuomo and Mayor Bloomberg are counting on the federal government to cover the tab, a heavy lift at a time of budget battles in Washington.

"Forty-billion dollars to try to finance through taxes would incapacitate the state," warned Cuomo, who met with the city's congressional delegation to discuss the figures.

And New York isn't alone in seeking federal help. New Jersey Gov. Chris Christie estimated the damage caused by Sandy in the Garden State at $29.4 billion.

Bloomberg headed to Washington to try to convince congressional leaders the city needs about $15 billion to be made whole, including $9.8 billion

more than what's usually provided by FEMA.

Officials said the NYPD anticipated spending $100 million on overtime; the Transportation Department planned $800 million in street repairs and $54 million to fix bridges; and the Parks Department was looking at $150 million to repair Rockaway Beach and another $30 million to restore Coney Island's beach.

Unexpected spending by all city agencies was estimated at $4.5 billion. Uninsured private losses were put at $4.8 billion, and $5.7 billion was claimed in lost business.

"The city will struggle to recover in the long term unless expedited federal funding is supplied," the mayor said in a press release, noting that Congress had allocated $120 billion after Katrina struck.

The mayor also told landlords of apartment buildings still without heat or electricity that the city is prepared to step in and make repairs they'll have to pay for if they don't sign up for no-cost fixes financed by FEMA.

He estimated that about 20,000 to 25,000 residents are still are without power.

Meanwhile, two executives with Long Island Power Authority — which has been heavily criticized for its storm response — have resigned. X. Cristofer Damianos, a member of the Board of Trustees, and Bruce Germano, vice president of customer service, both claimed their decisions had nothing to do with the outrage directed at LIPA. ■

New York Governor Andrew Cuomo speaks with the media in Long Beach, New York, on Oct. 31. Cuomo's office estimated the cost of Sandy's damage to New York State at $42 billion. (AP Images)

WAITING IN GAS LINES
NOW A 'FUEL'-TIME JOB

Demand for Gasoline Far Exceeds Supply

By Matt McNulty, Amy Stretten and Chuck Bennett

People stand in line for gas at the Hess station on Brooklyn's Fourth Avenue on Nov. 2. The station was one of the few in the city with fuel and power. (N.Y. Post: Spencer Burnett)

Desperate drivers waited in hours-long lines for gasoline in the days following Hurricane Sandy — as officials warned that it would still be several days before supplies get back to normal.

About half of the city's 242 gas stations had lines that extended for blocks, with motorists trying to fuel their cars and people trying to fill jugs.

At the Hess station on Fourth Avenue in Sunset Park, Brooklyn, there were cars in a 10-block line from 30th to 39th streets, and a second block-long line for emergency vehicles.

And in a third line, 80 people lined up about 100-feet long to pump fuel into canisters.

"We're not 100 percent sure when the system will be up and running where you won't feel any effect whatsoever," Gov. Cuomo said.

He urged New Yorkers not to drive if they didn't need to.

There "are continuing issues with the fuel delivery and distribution system," Cuomo said, adding it's a "short-term" problem because fuel deliveries are resuming.

Still, two New Jersey refineries and 10 regional petroleum terminals remain offline, according to the Department of Energy.

The demand was so desperate that some opportunists on Craigslist offered a gallon of fuel for $20 — and some gas stations imposed limits on how much customers could buy.

"We waited for two hours, and we were almost at the front of the line when they cut it off," said Miguel Mejia, at the Hess station in Sunset Park.

Some motorists were luckier.

"They ran out before we could fill up the tank, so we only got $21 worth, but that will last awhile," said Jeremy Ranieri. "The guy before me only got 45 cents before it shut off on him."

He and fiancée Amber Fox bought cookies for the cops and National Guardsmen maintaining order and fueling up emergency vehicles.

In New Jersey — where gas is being rationed by license-plate numbers — Homeland Security Secretary Janet Napolitano told residents that as electricity comes online, more fuel will be available.

"A lot of power has been restored. A lot remains to be restored," Napolitano said. ■

Part 2

BROOKLYN & QUEENS

A car in Brooklyn's Park Slope neighborhood was crushed by a tree that fell as superstorm Sandy ravaged New York. (N.Y. Post: Spencer Burnett)

THE MARINES

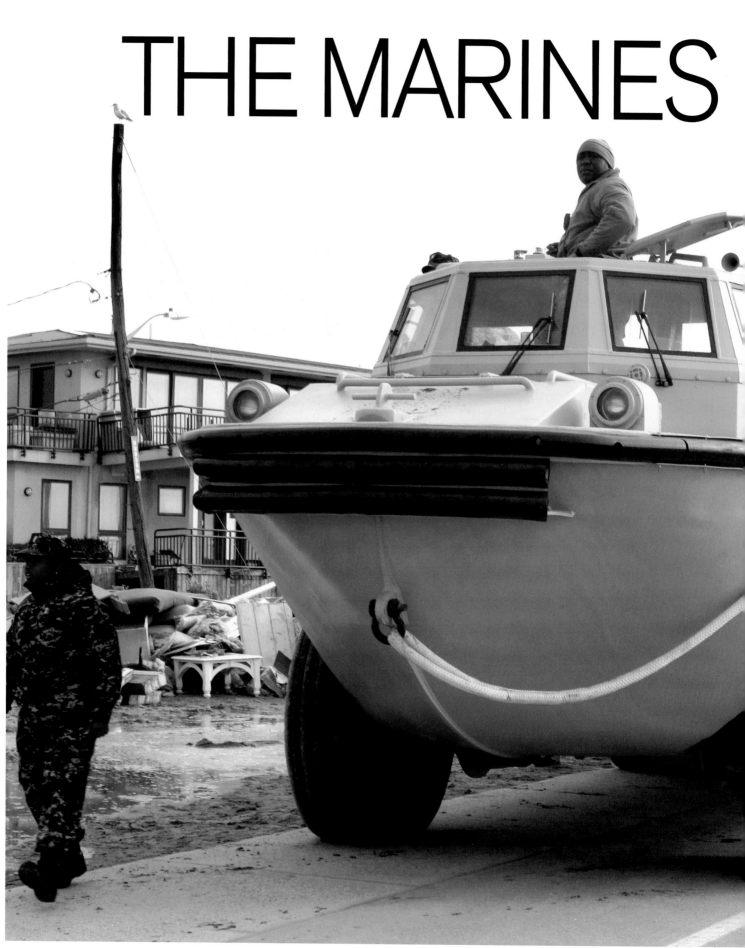

HAVE LANDED!

By Josh Margolin, Sally Goldenberg and Leonard Greene

Relief Reinforcements Come to the Rescue

They're storming the beaches! A wave of Marines hit the most hurricane-battered sections of Queens and Staten Island on Sunday, November 4, to bring much-needed assistance and supplies to increasingly desperate residents.

Armed with high-powered water pumps and sophisticated surveying equipment, the Leathernecks, aided by Navy sailors, began their attack on floodwaters from Rockaway Beach in Queens to Midland Beach on Staten Island.

"It's what Marines do. They just go running," said Marine Sgt. Justin Armstrong, who returned from Afghanistan about two months ago.

"It's pretty nasty," he said of the Rockaway wreckage. "It's a lot of sewage. Pretty much anything you'd flush down the toilet, that lays on the ground, that's trash. It's pretty vile stuff."

His work was appreciated.

"I was just speechless when I saw them," said Priscilla Smalls, 53, who lives in the Ocean Bay Houses in the Rockaways' Arverne section.

"I've never seen Marines anywhere before, let alone over here in the projects. It's a great, cool thing. We need the big guns after what happened here. I've seen the National Guard, but the Marines are a whole different thing."

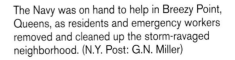

The Navy was on hand to help in Breezy Point, Queens, as residents and emergency workers removed and cleaned up the storm-ravaged neighborhood. (N.Y. Post: G.N. Miller)

"You've got several people who have had their houses totally robbed. The police were hopelessly overwhelmed in the first few days."
—Queens Councilman James Sanders

Marine engineers did a block-by-block assessment of Staten Island's Father Capodanno Boulevard to determine the manpower and equipment required for 50 to 100 more corps members to come ashore.

Meanwhile, Marines and Navy sailors were hard at work with hammers and hacksaws, doing any construction and cleanup they could.

"It was wonderful to see them," said Jessie Gonzalez, 34, whose home on nearby Patterson Avenue was flooded after the storm.

"They gave us supplies, water and food. It makes us feel like we're actually getting help now. At least we feel safer with their presence."

Residents felt similar relief in the Rockaways, where engineer and utilities Marines from the 8th Engineer Support Battalion drove up from Camp Lejeune, NC.

They started working at 5 a.m. at the Ocean Bay Houses with 150-gallon-per-minute pumps in what was likely to be a weeks-long effort to remove the chest-high water from the basements of the complex's 34 buildings.

Critics have complained that the National Guard's talents are being wasted. Instead of providing security against looters and directing traffic, they say, it's been ordered to do little more than give out food and blankets.

Sources said the Guard's role has been a source of contention between Mayor Bloomberg, who believes police have the situation under control, and Gov. Cuomo, who wants to blanket the area with the citizen soldiers.

"This thing goes back to the beginning of the storm," said a source working with city and state officials.

"The mayor downplayed it, and so he needs to keep maintaining the optics that it's not as bad by downplaying it. Bringing in the National Guard says that it's a major disaster because it is. It's bad. It's really bad. And Cuomo knows it."

Councilman James Sanders (D-Queens) griped, "You've got several people who have had their houses totally robbed. The police were hopelessly overwhelmed in the first few days."

In other developments:

- City officials warned that temperatures could dip below freezing and urged storm victims to seek refuge with friends or family or at government centers.

- The NYPD sent scores of cops to storm-ravaged areas to stand sentry in clusters of three or four to ward off looters. It also erected light towers to provide electricity to residents needing to charge phones or other devices.

- Most schools were set to reopen. Students were urged to dress warmly because some facilities are still without heat.

- Trash is being picked up, but regular schedules on Staten Island and in the Rockaways are impossible given the enormity of the debris, officials said. Trash from Breezy Point, Queens, was dumped in the Jacob Riis Park parking lot, sources said.

- Yankee Stadium has been converted to a storing house for donations and supplies for the National Guard to distribute.

- Retired NYPD cop Michael Dyer became just one more example of New Yorkers' altruistic spirit, driving a truck packed with 300 blankets from his home in Omaha, Neb., to the city's needy.

- Four police stations in Coney Island, Rockaway and on the Lower East Side were severely damaged by the storm. One of them, Brooklyn's 60th Precinct station, was evacuated. It's operating out of a temporary headquarters vehicle out front.

- City sanitation worker Michael Lewery was zapped by electricity while removing debris on Staten Island. The 13-year veteran was taken to Staten Island University North Hospital, where he was in stable condition, the department said. ∎

Additional reporting by Kate Kowsh, Reuven Fenton, Jennifer Bain and Jessica Simeone

With Old Glory flying where a house once stood, residents and emergency workers cleaned up the storm-ravaged Breezy Point neighborhood in early November. (N.Y. Post: G.N. Miller)

FOREVER SCARRED BY SANDY

By Jill Priluck

Storm Claims a Few New York Treasures

She was a once-in-a-century storm, but in terms of lost memories and destroyed treasures, Sandy was forever. It obliterated New Jersey's historic boardwalks and wrecked Long Island's power lines. Its floodwaters inundated downtown Manhattan and filled subway and traffic tunnels. Its 13-foot surge unleashed the ocean on thousands of homes in the Rockaways and Staten Island.

The Oct. 28-29 superstorm claimed 43 lives in New York City and wreaked some of the worst human suffering and property damage ever witnessed here.

From Gerritsen Beach to Pelham Bay, the hurricane uprooted as many as 40,000 people. Sandy devoured more than 8,000 street trees alone. Hundreds of homes burned down or were swept away, and tens of thousands need emergency repairs.

But most of the subways and tunnels are back, power is flowing, and tough-as-nails New Yorkers are rebuilding their homes and lives.

Yet full recovery may never be possible for these New York City icons:

Several sacred scrolls and holy books stored at the Brooklyn's Friends of Refugees of Eastern Europe Synagogue and Community Center were damaged by Sandy's floodwaters. Senior Rabbi Hershel Okonov (center) and his sons Rabbi Dovid Okonov (right) and Rabbi Avremel Okonov (left) roll a water-damaged Torah. (AP Images)

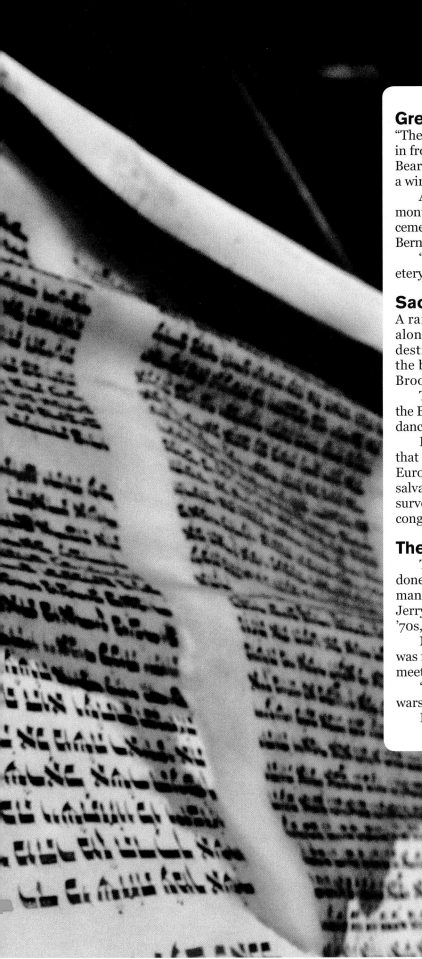

Green–Wood Cemetery's Angel

"The Lloyd Angel" — a 150-year-old marble statue in front of 19th-century painter William Holbrook Beard's burial plot — lost its head, an arm and part of a wing in the 90-mph gusts.

About 150 trees were uprooted, and at least 100 monuments were maimed in Brooklyn's 174-year-old cemetery, the resting place of Boss Tweed, Leonard Bernstein, Louis Comfort Tiffany and Horace Greeley.

"It's the worst we've seen in 40 years," said cemetery President Richard Moylan.

Sacred scrolls, Brighton Beach

A rare Babylonian Talmud printed in the 1800s — along with two sacred 50-year-old Torahs — were destroyed when floodwaters breached a safe in the basement of a synagogue in Brighton Beach, Brooklyn.

The damaged holy book, printed in Lithuania in the Babylonian form, has now been buried in accordance with Jewish law.

It was one of 115 prayer books and other texts that rabbis at the Friends of Refugees of Eastern Europe Synagogue and Community Center could not salvage in the wreckage. A Crown Heights scribe is surveying the damaged torahs, and it could cost the congregation thousands of dollars to save them.

The Shore Theater sign, Coney Island

The red and yellow sign that adorned the abandoned Shore Theater on Surf Avenue since 1925 was mangled. The theater once hosted Al Jolson and Jerry Lewis, but it had fallen into disrepair since the '70s, when it was an X-rated-movie house.

Nearby, another icon, the SpookARama ride, was flooded — with its Dracula and other attractions meeting a ghastly end.

"They've survived terrorist attacks and world wars, but not Sandy," co-owner Dennis Vourderis said. ∎

A section of a water-damaged Torah dries at the Friends of Refugees of Eastern Europe Synagogue and Community Center in Brooklyn's Crown Heights neighborhood. Several of the center's texts were damaged or destroyed by Sandy. (AP Images)

GLORY
HALLELUJAH

By Reuven Fenton, Beth Defalco and Dan MacLeod

Breezy Pointers Return and Vow to Rebuild

B reezy Point residents pledged to rebuild their community on Wednesday, Oct. 31, a day after it was ravaged by an inferno. Their spirit of hope was buoyed by an American flag that now flies over the neighborhood. It was found under rubble by a teenage girl.

"We were all in shock. How could that survive? When I saw it, I knew that everyone would be able to get through this and rebuild," 16-year-old Jacqueline Lacovara told the Post.

Lacovara, her family and neighbor Shamus Barnes hung the flag on the only thing left of Barnes' home — the metal frame from his awning.

"It was a little scarred, but otherwise untouched and unburned," Barnes said. "We put the flag up to bring a little hope."

The homes lost by Barnes and Lacovara — like those of many of their neighbors—had been in their families for 40-plus years.

Many returned to view their charred possessions.

"Our community is so close-knit," said Linda Strong, 59, who has lived in her Ocean Avenue house for 37 years. She vowed, "We'll all be a family again."

Marie Lopresti, a 72-year-old widow, stared at her home of 34 years and said, "It can be rebuilt. It's what we had inside — all our clothes, my husband's flag, all our memories.

"It meant nothing when I had it, but now it means everything."

"We're going to rebuild," said Lucille Dwyer, 64, who lived in her house for 23 years.

"You can't replace everything — all the sentimental things. I had photos of my son when he was a baby."

The blaze, whipped by winds generated by Hurricane Sandy, destroyed 111 houses and damaged scores more.

Frustrated volunteer firefighters saw the blaze start at around 8:15 p.m. Monday, but had no way of getting there because flooding had turned the streets into rivers.

"We could see the glow of the fire," said volunteer Michael Scotko, 23. "It was just hard knowing there was a fire but there being no way you could get there." ■

Local residents returned to the fire-ravaged Breezy Point section of Queens on Oct. 31, raising an American flag on the ruins of their home. The flag was found under the rubble. (Getty Images)

NABE THE CITY 'FORGOT'

By Jennifer Bain and Leonard Greene

Gloom in Gerritsen Beach

At age 80, George Broadhead is old enough to remember the days when the tiny bungalows in Gerritsen Beach used piles of coal for heat. "If we ran out of coal, it was a big deal," Broadhead said. "My mother would say, 'You can wear your clothes to bed.' Now, here I am all these years later wearing my clothes to bed because it's so cold."

Day 11 passed on Thursday, Nov. 8, with no heat or electricity in this forgotten Brooklyn bailiwick.

What was once a charming enclave — a "seashore in the city," one Realtor said — had become a virtual war zone, a place where a bomb was dropped.

Homeowner Kathy Ene says the city should have seen it coming.

This peninsula in southeast Brooklyn practically floods on a cloudy day, yet when the fire-breathing Hurricane Sandy bore down on New York, Gerritsen Beach was designated a "B" zone, which meant evacuations weren't mandated.

"We do feel neglected," Ene said. "The Red Cross didn't get here until Friday, and all they did was hand out hot chocolate and blankets. We have no electricity down here. The place is a ghost town. It's black, total blackness.

"It feels like a war zone. We understand how those people abandoned in Katrina feel."

Ene's Garland Court home was flooded with four feet of water. She and her husband, Dan, have spent the days since dumping ruined furniture and rusted appliances.

"Fifteen years of memories," she said, her voice breaking like a windswept tree branch. "I never thought this would be me."

Streets that were once dirt roads are piled high with storm debris. Mold is eating away at sheetrock that wasn't washed away in homes. Those lucky enough to have their cars spared by the apocalyptic storm can't find gas for miles.

Restoring power here is more than fixing power lines and flipping a switch.

Basement electrical boxes in hundreds of homes were ruined by saltwater and must be replaced before power can be turned back on. Each job takes hours to complete, and city officials have to sign off on each repair.

"We need a better coordinated effort," said state Sen. Martin Golden (R-Brooklyn). "If you don't do that, we'll be having this conversation in December."

"Gerritsen Beach has been forgotten," said Linda Barone D'Arrigo. ∎

Upended and sunk boats lined Brooklyn's Gerritsen Beach on Nov. 3 following Hurricane Sandy. More than a week passed before power was restored to the area. (AP Images)

PLUCKED FROM **PERIL**

By Cynthia Fagen

Greenpoint Couple Rescues Chicken

A Greenpoint couple waiting out Hurricane Sandy at their local pub took a stray chicken under their wing. Chris Mottalini, 33, and his girlfriend, Nepal Asatthawa, 31, had been putting back some beers when they spotted a brown chicken clucking and strutting in front of the bar.

Worried that the hen would become a victim of the looming "Frankenstorm," the pair picked the gentle bird up and took it home with them.

There, they made her a bed from a cardboard box and lined it with T-shirts to make her comfortable in the kitchen as the hurricane approached.

"She was so freaked out by the storm, she wouldn't stop clucking," said Mottalini.

On Tuesday, the no-longer-spooked hen showed her thanks by laying them an egg.

"She's a good girl," said Mottalini, who's sending her to a new home at the Farm Sanctuary in Watkins Glen, NY.

"We have the egg in the fridge," he said. "We just would feel bad about cooking it while she was here." ∎

Chris Mottalini and girlfriend Nepal Asatthawasi pose with "FrankenHen" the brown chicken they saved during the storm in Brooklyn's Greenpoint neighborhood. (N.Y. Post: Cynthia Fagen)

VODKA WITH A TWISTER

Bar Washes Up on Block

By Kenneth Garger, Dana Sauchelli and Rich Calder

The drinks were on Sandy! A Brooklyn marina pub broke off from its main structure during the hurricane — and floated two miles before landing on a residential street, treating stunned residents there to its well-stocked bar for an after-storm bash.

"We had a big party. We had nothing else to do while we were waiting for everything else to dry, and this was a great opportunity to get our minds off everything," said Michael Sarrell, 27, one of the Gerritsen Beach residents who took solace in the battered Gateway Marina bar that came to rest just outside their door.

The bar — which residents identified as a chunk of the marina establishment on federal parkland on Flatbush Avenue — had been lifted from its foundation in Mill Basin during Superstorm Sandy and drifted in swollen Deep Creek Bay, past the Belt Parkway, all the way west to the dead-end block at Madoc Avenue and Keen Court in Gerritsen Beach.

"It was moving 30 mph toward my house!" said Patrice Dolan, 52, who recalled screaming, "Oh, my God! What do I do? What do I do?" as the surreal moment played out.

When the bar hut came to a rest, residents discovered its tables and chairs were miraculously intact — as was a wide variety of booze.

By Wednesday, residents had set up an impromptu watering hole, writing "SANDY'S BAR" in red marker across the gray facade.

Once the liquor supply quickly ran out, "B.Y.O.B." was scribbled below.

Sarrell's brother Keith, 26, said the whole neighborhood then took to bringing in booze, coolers and even power generators to keep the party going.

"We had Jameson, Skyy Vodka and a bunch of beer," said resident Nino Coppolino, 29. "We packed 40 people in there. That's a lot of body heat to stay warm."

The partying lasted through the evening of Friday, Nov. 6, but ended the next day, when cops and sanitation workers arrived and razed the structure for safety reasons.

"I was going to try and put it in my back yard and make it a permanent bar, but they had to knock it down," Keith Sarrell said.

By Monday night, with the bar gone and reality setting in, residents along the strip were burning damaged furniture and cardboard in a barrel to keep warm.

It's unclear when the devastated seaside community will get its power back.

Bill Gallucci, a 50-year-old boat mechanic, said the liquor license on one of the displaced bar's walls indicated it was part of Gateway Marina.

The structure "had thousands of dollars of floatation devices under it," he said. "And they had barnacles growing on them."

Some residents had briefly believed the bar was actually part of a popular beach bar in Breezy Point, Queens, seven miles away called the Sugar Bowl because the structures looked similar.

"It's a shame they had to tear it down," Gallucci said of the hut. "It probably could've been transported safely back to the marina." ∎

"Sandy's Bar" became a party spot after Sandy tore it from its Mill Basin foundation and carried it – its booze intact – two miles to Gerritsen Beach. (James Messerschmidt)

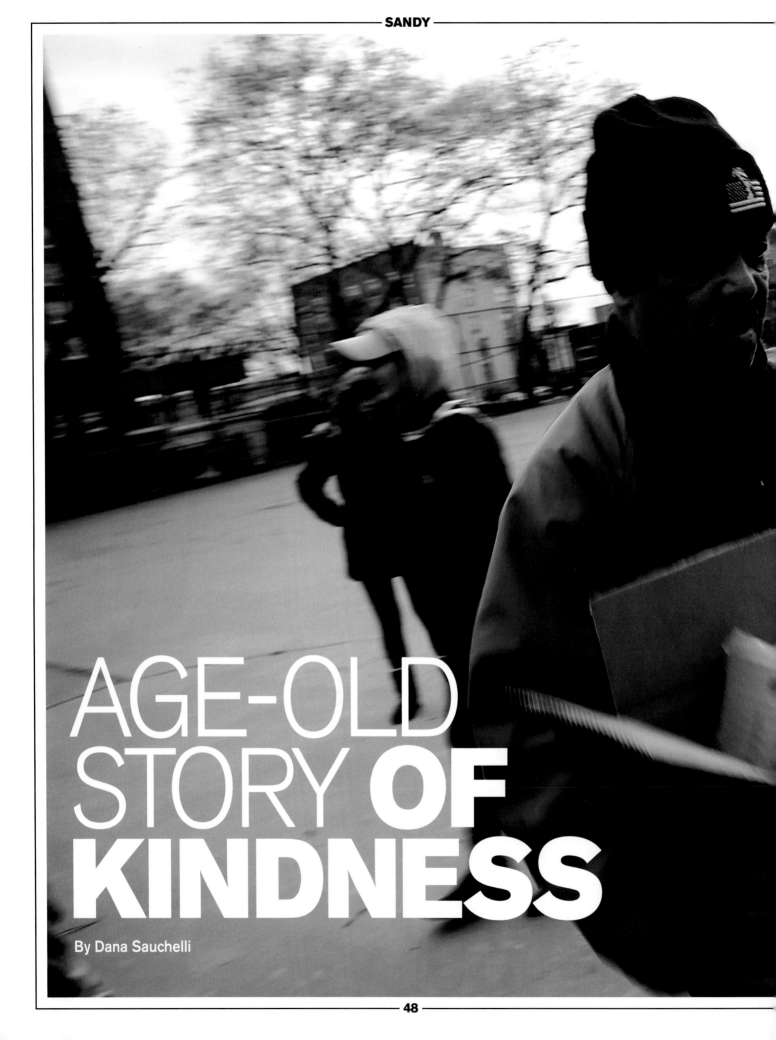

AGE-OLD STORY **OF** KINDNESS

By Dana Sauchelli

Strangers Care for Elderly Neighbors

I n Red Hook, the west side of the neighborhood was still without power, with elderly residents essentially trapped inside of their apartments. Dorothy Robinson, 94, stayed in her fifth-floor apartment on Center Mall in the Red Hook Houses.

"I've seen worse. World War II was worse," Robinson said.

"But I didn't think it was going to be this bad."

Three days after the storm, she was running out of food, as was Joshua Rodney, who's also on the fifth floor.

Rodney, 85, has a leg injury and breathing problems. "God, oh mercy, I can't go down the stairs," Rodney said.

Both relied on the kindness of strangers, and those strangers were reliable. On Nov. 1, volunteer Conor Tomas Reed, 31, of the Red Hook Initiative, brought plates of rice, beans and vegetables, along with gallons of water for residents.

When Reed asked Robinson if she'd be needing him the next day, she jumped at the chance. "Yes," she said. "Please come back tomorrow."

Many of the hardest hit from the power, water and phone outages were the elderly, who suffered particularly in the taller buildings of Manhattan, Brooklyn and Staten Island.

More than 500 evacuees from blacked-out nursing homes wound up at the Brooklyn Armory. "No, no, I don't like it here," Michael Downing, 52, a wheelchair-bound refugee from the Central Manor Home for Adults in Far Rockaway, said. ∎

A resident of Brooklyn's Red Hook Houses receives donated water and ready-to-eat meals on Nov. 2. Several good Samaritans helped residents of the apartment building, which was without water and power for days following superstorm Sandy. (Getty Images)

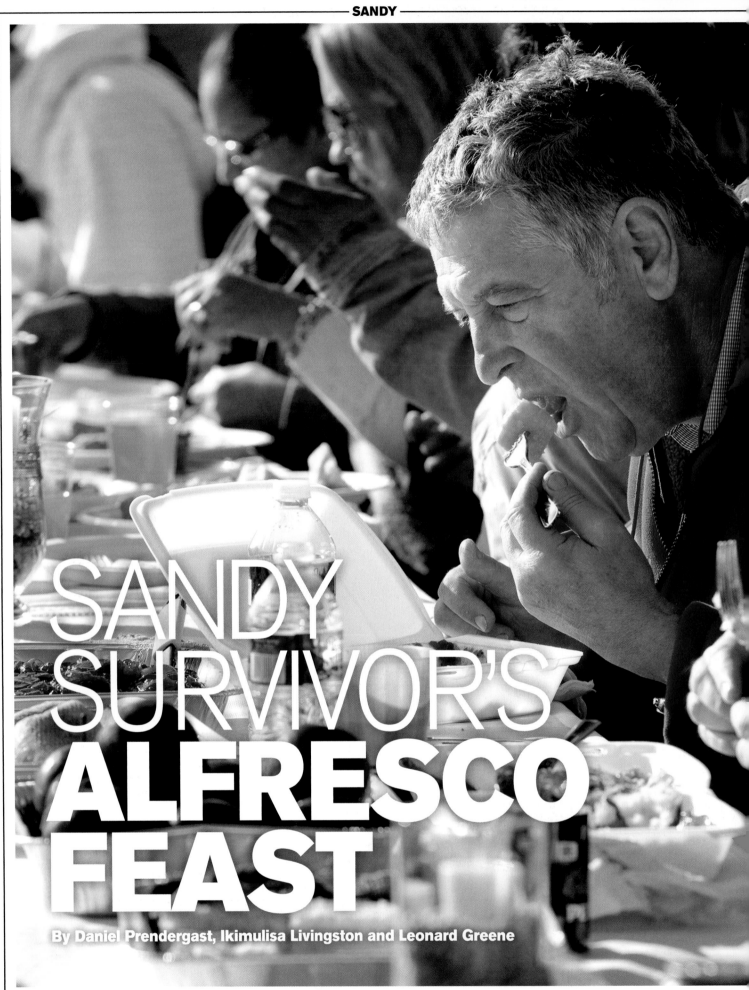

SANDY SURVIVOR'S ALFRESCO FEAST

By Daniel Prendergast, Ikimulisa Livingston and Leonard Greene

Those Worst Hit Resourcefully Celebrate Thanksgiving

They stumbled in the dark for weeks, their homes are filled with mold, and looters are lurking — but Sandy survivors were determined to enjoy Thanksgiving.

"I lost everything, but we're still alive," said Rockaway Beach resident Louis DeCarolis, 51. "So there's a lot to be thankful for."

DeCarolis took the resourceful approach to Thanksgiving. With no electricity to power his oven, he dropped 80 pounds of charcoal in a pit he dug in his front yard and earlier this week cooked two turkeys on a makeshift grill.

On Wednesday, his power came back on. He cooked outside anyway.

"We had decided already," DeCarolis said. "We made up our minds even with the lights back on."

And survivors in wrecked Brooklyn neighborhoods seemingly forgotten by politicians — like Manhattan Beach and Red Hook — also made the best of holiday.

Patrick Cavanaugh continues to deal with flood damage to his Manhattan Beach home, but still he hosted Thanksgiving dinner last night for family.

Over turkey and stuffing, they talked about how it feels to be forgotten.

"People got destroyed here, but you didn't hear a word about it," Cavanaugh said. "I mean, it was like a Third World country here.

"But no politicians came here. No one from the Red Cross was here. It was like we were forgotten about."

In Red Hook, Justo Lugo, 49, accepted a hot turkey dinner from Red Cross volunteer Judy Malpass, 66.

"This is nice what they're doing," said Lugo, who lives in a seventh-floor apartment at the Red Hook Houses. "God knows I'm hungry."

Mayor Bloomberg spent part of his holiday with firefighters in Far Rockaway preparing dinner for the firehouse.

"Given the size of the storm and the fires and that sort of thing, we're really lucky we didn't have that many people that died," Bloomberg said. ∎

Carlos Buti (center) and others share a free Thanksgiving dinner in the Rockaway area of the Queens. Many homes in the heavily-damaged area were still without power weeks after Sandy. (AP Images)

Part 3

STATEN ISLAND

An Oct. 31 helicopter view shows the damage to Staten Island's shore. Several boats washed ashore and buildings were damaged as stormwaters and winds crippled the island. (N.Y. Post: Matthew McDermott)

ISLAND OF
DESPAIR

How a Deadly Mix of Complacency and Defiance Sank Sleepy Staten

By Brad Hamilton and Candice M. Giove

After waiting until 9 p.m. on Monday, Oct. 29, to respond to warnings about the storm, Glenda Moore hastily strapped her two young boys into car seats, packed their Halloween costumes into the family's Ford Explorer and sped from her home on Staten Island toward Brooklyn.

Fleeing the hard-hit neighborhood of Great Kills, she planned to cross the Verrazano Bridge and take refuge at her mother's house, but on Father Capodanno Boulevard, Sandy's surge swamped the SUV, pushing it into the mud.

Moore jumped from the stalled SUV with Connor, 4, and Brandon, 2, and carried them to a tree, then to a house, where she pounded on a door.

"She's struggling, and the owner didn't answer," said a city official who spoke to Moore.

She went around back. Desperate and in thigh-high water, she picked up a clay pot, planning to break a window. But in that moment, she loosened her grip on the kids and they were swept away by the raging brown foam.

Moore called out to them throughout the night, screaming in the dark for hours. Cops found the tiny bodies three days later, in a swollen marsh a quarter-mile away.

The two boys were among 22 people who died on the South Shore of Staten Island — more than half of the city's entire tragic toll of 43. Because of ignored evacuation warnings and poor flood planning, the least populous borough paid a high price during the hurricane's rampage.

Other communities, particularly the Rockaways, were hammered by the storm, but none suffered as badly as Staten Island. Hundreds of neat, winterized bungalows were reduced to rubble in Midland, South and Oakwood beaches and Ocean Breeze.

"People are rummaging through garbage where their houses used to be," said Charlene Wagner, district manager of Community Board 3.

"The only time I've seen devastation like this," said City Councilman James Oddo, "is in the movies."

In the days before the storm, there were repeated dire warnings — and much skepticism — in these communities, populated by blue-collar workers and city employees, many of whom pulled around-the-clock shifts to see New York through Sandy.

Their aging, one-floor bungalows, wedged between the soft sand and marshland, are now dwarfed by new, sturdier McMansions. Few residents enjoy sweeping views of the Verrazano Narrows Bridge, but all can walk a few blocks to the miles-long FDR Boardwalk and Midland Beach promenade to relish the wide beaches, salty air and spectacular vistas.

It's a slice of the city that's unfamiliar to many New Yorkers.

It was once a summer playground and featured first-rate hotels and amusements. But mostly this

Matthew Emanuel takes a photo of a sailboat that washed ashore in his yard on Tuesday, Oct. 30. in the Midland Beach neighborhood of Staten Island. (N.Y. Post: Chad Rachman)

was where working immigrants settled — the Irish in Midland Beach and Italians in South Beach.

"These are small communities — mom-and-pops, little houses, firemen, policemen," said Borough President James Molinaro. "This is the middle class of America, right here."

It's also one of the city's most vulnerable areas. Most of the island sits at or below sea level, and storm surges have long plagued its shores. City and federal plans to protect Staten Island from water have been in play for more than 50 years — with little to show for it.

In 1960, a study by the Army Corp of Engineers led to a $9 million blueprint to build dunes, levees and stone jetties from Fort Wadsworth to Tottenville, a 13 miles stretch of the eastern and southern coast. Work was set to begin in 1965. It never happened.

"They're going to have to answer for what happened to those plans," Oddo said.

In 1979, the city put in a new storm sewer system that helped reduce flooding, and in 1992 a berm was built to protect Oakwood Beach. But the ambitious "Bluebelt" plan — where the city preserves and tailors existing ponds and wetlands to soak up storm and floodwater — has never reached its full potential.

Still, Staten Islanders had not seen a truly devastating storm hit its semi-sheltered shores since the 1992 nor'easter. And in 2011, according to elected leaders, an air of invincibility followed Hurricane Irene.

Residents were told to prepare for disaster, but the storm passed relatively quietly.

"Nothing happened," recalled Midland Beach resident Joseph Herrnkind, 50. "The weathermen cry wolf so many times."

Seven days before it struck New York, Sandy took shape as a tropical storm in Jamaica before churning up the Eastern Seaboard.

Experts soon realized that a rare convergence of weather could turn it into a monster. The hurricane and two other storm fronts from the north and south were converging, and the "Frankenstorm" was

A helicopter view shows homes along the Staten Island coast that were washed away by superstorm Sandy. (N.Y. Post: Matthew McDermott)

set to arrive at high tide, which would be two feet higher than normal because of a full moon.

What scared them most was that a wall of high pressure in the north Atlantic could force the storm sharply northwest — a big hook swinging straight at the city.

"She kind of got stuck in the worst possible place," said Dan Hofmann, meteorologist with National Weather Service.

"It looked like it was almost heading out safely to sea, but then that hard left happens first thing Monday morning, and that's when things started to go bad."

While Irene struck at a glancing blow, Sandy came directly at New York. When she arrived at about 8 p.m. on Monday, Oct. 29, the storm tore into Staten Island head on, pushing a 13½-foot-high tidal surge.

Yet many simply thumbed their noses at the looming threat.

Molinaro said that during a tour of shelters, he was shocked to see row after row of empty cots. At the Todt Hill facility, "there were 43 people there and they had cots for 400," he said.

Thousands of people — all in the shore's mandatory evacuation zone — simply refused to go.

"We had a hurricane party," said Teresa Guido of Midland Beach, who invited guests for dinner and wine.

The festivities were soon over when a wall of water came crashing in.

"Cars that were parked here washed down the block," she said of Father Capodanno Boulevard.

Bill Kruger, of Quincy Avenue in Ocean Breeze, was in his house listening to a radio broadcast by the mayor when suddenly his wife, Rose, ran downstairs to the basement, hoping to protect their wedding album.

"All of a sudden, I heard a loud crash," he recalled.

"Rose, now!" he screamed. "We got to go now!" She came up the stairs just as the surge walloped their basement.

Police respond to a possible water rescue as waves crash on shore in Staten Island's Huguenot neighborhood on Monday, Oct. 29, 2012, just hours before Hurricane Sandy made landfall. (N.Y. Post: Chad Rachman)

"These are small communities— mom-and-pops, little houses, firemen, policemen. This is the middle class of America, right here."

—Staten Island Borough President James Molinaro

"It was a matter of three seconds that she turned that corner," he said.

Not everyone was so lucky.

Ella Norris, 89, succumbed to hypothermia in her daughter's arms after icy, chest-deep waters flooded their home in Ocean Breeze. John Filipow-icz, 51, and his 20-year-old son, John, of Oakwood Beach died in their basement, their bodies locked in embrace.

When storm waters swamped her bungalow home on Grimsby Street in Midland Beach, Lucy Spagnuolo's first thought was to get her 80-year-old mom, Beatrice, out.

So she told her to put on her boots and wait. "Ma, Let me pull up the car," the postal worker said.

But after trekking to her Cadillac sedan through knee-deep water, Spagnuolo watched in horror as a power line hit the water.

"I was afraid that I would get electrocuted."

So she drove to her boyfriend's house for help.

On their way back, still blocks away, the couple spotted cops and begged them to rescue Beatrice.

"They said, 'It's too dangerous. No one is al-lowed in.'" And they were allowed no further.

Police did not reach the house until 2 p.m. the next day. They discovered Beatrice dead, sitting in a chair, the high water line above her head.

Her next-door neighbor, Anastasia Rispoli, 73, was also found dead.

The push of water was a lethal surprise —

waves were high enough to reach the top of one-story houses. The mix of water and falling trees knocked out power to 133,000 of 174,000 Con Ed customers on the island.

By early Tuesday, Oct. 30, Staten Island — long called the "forgotten borough" by its 450,000 resi-dents — was devastated.

Rescue workers had been out within hours of the storm's arrival, but no relief came to the newly homeless. Food, water and clothing were lacking.

On Thursday, Nov. 1, elected officials toured the area, and a handful of Federal Emergency Manage-ment Agency workers offered phones to residents. The National Guard set up in New Dorp Beach with food, water and blankets. On Friday, FEMA opened a help center, and Red Cross workers showed up. None had information about shelters.

Even so, victims had to rely more on each other than from relief agencies.

"I have nothing," said South Beach resident Jadwiga Lynko, whose house was destroyed.

She survived the storm by balancing herself on top of her kitchen sink for six hours — and praying.

Will Staten Island be better prepared for the next storm?

Many aren't sure.

"People chose to live by the water," said Den-nis Laurie, an EMT who lost his home in Ocean Breeze. "It's a chance you're going to take. You just cross your fingers and pray." ∎

Amanda Pero, 25, clings to a warning-flag pole in blustery Midland Beach, Staten Island, on Oct. 29. (NY Post: Chad Rachman)

SAD EMPTY SEATS

By Joe Tacopino, Jessica Simeone and Pedro Oliveira Jr.

Staten Island Children Swept Away as Mother Fled for Safety

A massive search involving dozens of rescuers was conducted for two Staten Island boys who were swept from their mother's arms by fierce floodwaters. The boys — Connor, 4, and Brandon, 2 — went missing the evening of Monday, Oct. 29, while mother Glenda Moore, a nurse at Lutheran Medical Center in Brooklyn, made a desperate attempt to flee from her Great Kills home to Brooklyn.

Moore's Ford Explorer — packed with baby clothes, diaper bags and an umbrella — stalled on severely flooded Father Capodanno Boulevard in South Beach a few miles from her home. She got out of the car with the boys to ask for help.

By then, the waves were picking up speed and Moore lost her grip on toddler Brandon. The desperate mother clutched tighter to her older boy — but Connor, too, was swept away by the water.

She continued to search for the boys all night, knocking on neighboring houses for help, the children's grandfather said. The distraught mother got none.

"She spent all night on the steps outside," said the grandfather, who did not want to be identified. "Nobody wanted to help her."

The mother was finally able to get help the next morning, when she was taken to a local hospital with hypothermia.

Brandon and Connor Moore, ages 2 and 4, were sitting in their mother's Ford Explorer when their mom, terrified by the rising waters as they fled their home for higher ground, got out with them to ask for help. But the boys were swept away. (N.Y. Post: Chad Rachman)

"For all we do to recover, I think it's fair to say we can't replace the lives lost as a result the storm."

—New York Mayor Michael Bloomberg

"It was an absolute nightmare," said Iqbal Mughal, 46, a neighbor who rescued three other people stuck in the flood but did not hear or see Moore as she struggled to find her children.

"You couldn't hear anyone screaming because the waves were so loud," another neighbor explained.

"It's one experience in my life that I'll never forget," added a shaken Mughal, who housed nearly 30 neighbors in the second floor of his home, whose first floor was flooded by more than 5 feet of water.

Moore was taken home Oct. 31, where she reunited with her husband, Damien, a city sanitation worker who was in Brooklyn during his wife's harrowing search for Connor and Brandon.

Neighbors said the beloved parents looked "dazed."

"They are beautiful little guys," said neighbor Laurene Ryan, 62, of the boys. "I usually hear them playing in the yard. Connor always had a smiley face. They're such nice people.

"This is so wrong. This is just unbelievable. There are no words."

Another neighbor, Val Mironovich, 71, said, "They're the two nicest people that live on this block. They're very caring, hardworking people."

Nearly 40 rescuers focused on nearby marshes, into which Moore's SUV was pushed — and where the waves may have taken the children.

The search party carried pitchforks, shovels and wooden sticks to comb through the marshes, where water reached as high as 5 feet.

A helicopter equipped with a heat-seeking device hovered overhead, searching for any hints of life in the marshes. Rescuers aboard an airboat sifted through deeper waters for the kids.

Meanwhile, rescuers lifted debris and pulled out two other cars stuck in the marshes. A felled tree was removed.

Yet there was no sign of the two boys — and rescue efforts were suspended for the night.

The death toll from superstorm Sandy climbed yet again as rescuers continued to discover bodies in cars overtaken by flooding and debris-filled buildings throughout the city and the suburbs.

"For all we do to recover, I think it's fair to say we can't replace the lives lost as a result of the storm," Mayor Bloomberg said.

"And we may find a few more bodies," the mayor warned.

"Our hearts go out to families who lost loved ones and homes."

Throughout the country, at least 64 people were killed, including nine in Maryland, eight in New Jersey, six in Pennsylvania, five in West Virginia, four in Connecticut, two in Virginia and one in North Carolina.

One person was killed due to the storm in Toronto, Canada. Before reaching the United States, the storm had killed 69 people in the Caribbean.

The storm also killed a 24-year-old couple walking their dog in Brooklyn, a 29-year-old Queens groom-to-be, and two parents in New Jersey — who were crushed by a tree in front of their kids, ages 11 and 14. ■

Police use a swamp boat to search for two missing children in the South Beach neighborhood of Staten Island on Wednesday, Oct. 31. The children were swept away as their mother tried to escape the storm. The bodies of Connor and Brandon Moore were recovered a day later. (N.Y. Post: Chad Rachman)

STATEN ISLAND MOTHER'S FLOOD OF TEARS

Bodies of Surge-Swept Boys, 2 & 4, Are Found

By Doug Auer, Jessica Simeone and Leonard Greene

The nightmare that began when raging storm waters ripped two little Staten Island boys from their mother's arms reached its tragic conclusion when their bodies were found in marshlands close to where they disappeared.

Glenda Moore wailed uncontrollably after cops showed up at her Great Kills home and delivered the grim news.

The short lives of Brandon, 2, and Connor, 4, ended in murky water, under debris and trees toppled by the storm. They were found about 20 yards apart at around 10 a.m. on Nov. 1 by cops in wet suits using shovels and pitchforks to clear the thick brush.

"It's a shock for everybody right now," a family friend said outside the Brooklyn home where Moore retreated to the comfort of family members. "She's in pain."

Moore and her husband, Damien — a city sanitation worker who had been in Brooklyn during the hurricane — stopped at a funeral home to make arrangements for the boys, described by a friend as "the joy of their lives."

Brandon and Connor were separated from their mother as she frantically tried to lead them to safety, away from raging floodwaters brought by Hurricane Sandy.

"Terrible, absolutely terrible," Police Commissioner Ray Kelly said. "It compounds all the tragic aspects of this horrific event."

Moore's Ford Explorer had gotten stuck when she was separated from her boys, police said.

Officials said Moore became frightened when the storm hit, and she rushed out of the house en route to her mother's home in Brooklyn.

But the SUV, which she packed with a diaper bag, Halloween costumes and decorations, stalled along Father Capodanno Boulevard as the street began to flood.

After a panicked call to her husband, Moore grabbed Brandon and Connor and fled the SUV, but the rising water caused her to lose her grip as the boys drifted helplessly out of her reach.

Cops said Moore banged on the doors of nearby houses, desperately seeking help. But the people who answered turned her away. She had to ride out the storm outside and got no help until hours later, when rescuers found her clinging to a post on a porch.

Cops found the boys about 30 yards off the corner of McLaughlin Street and Father Capodanno Boulevard, law-enforcement sources said.

A neighbor said the family had been trying to move to Brooklyn in the weeks before the storm.

"The tolls are so high, and they both work there," said neighbor Anthony Monti, 72. "Everyone in the neighborhood likes them. They're really nice people. I'm going to light a candle when I go to church for those two boys."

The family friend in Brooklyn said: "Keep them in your prayers. They're going to need it. They were joyful kids, very happy." ■

Additional reporting by Larry Celona and Joe Tacopino

Glenda Moore leaves the scene where the bodies of her two children were found in the South Beach neighborhood of Staten Island. The two boys, ages 2 and 4, were found yards apart after being swept away in the Hurricane Sandy storm surge as they tried to flee. (NY Post: Chad Rachman)

DEATH'S DOORSTEP

Miracle he Survived, but his House Didn't

By Joe Tacopino and Beth DeFalco

He survived 9/11, fought in Iraq, and now guards killers at Sing Sing, but he's never been more scared than when Sandy came to his Staten Island doorstep.

"I made it through 9/11 when the second tower fell. I was there for the Baghdad invasion. I never thought I was gonna die," Pedro Correa said, until Oct. 29, when Sandy made landfall.

"That night, I thought I was gonna die."

As the storm hit, he sent his wife and children, ages 2 and 6, inland to safely, but Correa stayed behind to protect the Kissam Avenue home he'd remodeled in Oakwood Beach.

Heavy winds blew off the roof, and soon, the entire structure started to collapse. Then the floodwaters came.

He called his wife and son to say a final goodbye, then with a broken rib swam to a neighbor's house on Mill Road.

"How I survived that night — I go over it in my head a million times — I can't understand it," Correa told The Post, standing on the rubble that was his home.

A month later, Sandy had drained his wallet.

Correa estimates his house and possessions were worth about $600,000, but his insurance is capped at $250,000, and FEMA has offered only $2,800.

"I'm going to see a bankruptcy lawyer. I lost everything out here," Correa said.

He rented an apartment nearby so his children can stay in school, and he's looking to the government for help.

"I served my country. I served my state for a lot of years," he said.

Along with Correa, hundreds of thousands of people were still reeling from Sandy's aftermath one month later:

- LIPA reports 12,000 "customers" — which could be entire buildings — in Nassau, Suffolk and the Rockaways remained without power. About 1,600 Con Ed customers on Staten Island and in Brooklyn, Queens and Manhattan lacked electricity.

- More than 234,000 New Yorkers had contacted FEMA for assistance, and more than $690 million has been approved.

- Nearly 57,000 survivors had stayed at various recovery centers in the affected areas, and 34 centers remained open.

- 9,323 homes had registered for NYC's Rapid Repairs program — for heat, water and power— but through Nov. 28, only 817 were in the process of being repaired, and just 38 home repairs had been completed.

- The city was to offer a 90-day deferral of third-quarter property-tax bills for any unlivable home that had been red-tagged.

- Dozens of schools in the city and on Long Island canceled winter-break vacation days to make up for missed classes.

- The R train between Brooklyn and Manhattan was still not running, nor was the A train south of Howard Beach. ∎

Pedro Correa was lucky to be standing on Nov. 28 as he surveyed the grounds where his Staten Island house stood before Sandy destroyed it. (N.Y. Post: Chad Rachman)

PRESIDENT VISITS
DEVASTATION

Staten Island Man Bears His Pain to Obama

By Leonard Greene

Dominick Camerada is still waiting for the storm to pass. After the flood from Hurricane Sandy filled his Staten Island home with five feet of water, the car he bought his oldest son as a high-school graduation present floated four blocks away.

When Camerada finally got heat in his 30-degree New Dorp bedroom, Con Ed shut off the gas to his house because there was water in the main line. Then looters raided his shed and stole all his tools.

And, as if that weren't enough, in the midst of all the turmoil, his guy lost the big election — on his birthday.

Camerada, 50, is a fast talker. In an unplanned five-minute meeting on Thursday, Nov. 15, with the president of the United States — the president of the United States — the retired UPS worker managed to share his entire tale of hardship.

Well, almost the entire tale. That part about voting for the other guy he kept to himself.

"Did I vote for Obama?" Camerada said later, after the president's helicopter took off and whisked him back to Washington. "No, I didn't. I've been a Democrat all my life, a union guy, a shop steward. But I needed to send him a message. I knew he was going to win, but I wanted to give him a wakeup call."

But that was before the leader of the free world sauntered down Camerada's street, hugged his wife, Diane, like a church pastor would, and shook the father's hand and looked him in the eye.

And listened. Oh, he made a couple of speeches during the day, thanked hardworking relief workers, that sort of thing.

But with Camerada, the president listened. For five whole minutes.

That's more time than some Cabinet secretaries get.

"It gave me some kind of consolation," Camerada said.

"It's no easy thing to get on a helicopter and jump down in the middle of a disaster area."

The weary homeowner made the most of his meeting. He told the president of the United States that the $19,000 he was offered from FEMA for his family's pain and suffering was "a slap in the face."

"What would $19,000 do for anybody down here?"

He said he used those words.

"There's gotta be something you can do to make things right down here," one man told the other man.

"We had a heart to heart," Camerada said later. Obama didn't get Camerada's vote. But he

Dominick and Diane Comerada's home in Staten Island's New Dorp Beach neighborhood was filled with five feet of water when Sandy hit New York. (N.Y. Post: Chad Rachman)

"He's a human being. He felt my pain. I not only spoke for myself, but for my community."

—Dominick Camerada

might have earned something better. He got the voter's confidence.

"He's a human being. He felt my pain. I not only spoke for myself, but for my community," Camerada said.

"He said he would try to 'pass a law for more disaster funds.' He said he 'was going to try to make it right.'"

Camerada didn't pretend to know exactly what that meant.

He's also didn't pretend that he and his wife and their four boys were going to wake up the next day in the freezing, dark house where they have stayed since the hurricane and everything would be back to normal.

"I'm the only provider for my family," he said.

"You don't turn your back on your family. I spent almost every penny that I had. My whole life is invested in this house."

The storm was going to stay awhile.

But he could get out of the cold bed in the morning secure in the knowledge that after pulling out all the wet drywall, and finding new parts for the boiler, and stacking all the memories on the sidewalk, after all that, he could feel like he did his part because he shook another man's hand, looked him in the eye and did what any real man would do for his family and his community.

He asked for help. ∎

President Obama chats with Dominick and Diane Camerada during a tour of their devastated Staten Island neighborhood of New Dorp on Nov. 15. (N.Y. Post: Chad Rachman)

OBAMA GIFTS SHINE, BUT 1000s STILL OUT

By Dana Sauchelli

Sandy-Struck Family Gets Ornaments from White House

Most Christmas tree lights blink on and off — but incredibly, thousands of New Yorkers were still stuck completely in "off" on Christmas Day 2013 following Hurricane Sandy nearly two months earlier.

But in the areas hardest hit, the lights are slowly coming back — each a symbol of hope.

In Rockaway Park, power was finally restored yesterday to a 70-unit apartment building.

Until now, the residents had only partial power provided by generators.

"Before, it was candles, flashlights and takeout food," said Dennis Krecko, 57. "It was a nice Christmas present.

"I can live my life normally again," he said. "I can use the microwave. I can heat something in the toaster.

"Life is slowing coming back to Rockaway."

His tree sports ornaments cut by a neighbor from pieces of the destroyed boardwalk. They say "Hope" on one side and "2012" on the other.

More than 1,000 Con Ed customers remained without power in Brooklyn, Queens and Staten Island. LIPA said some 8,100 homes in the Rockaways were so badly damaged, they still couldn't accept electricity.

Meanwhile, Joe and Debbie Ingenito and their three children are among the lucky residents of Staten Island — their power is back and their lives have been brightened by President Obama's gift of two ornaments for their tree.

After The Post wrote about the makeshift Christmas tree that Joe had erected on his sidewalk

Joe Ingenito poses with the remains of his prized blue spruce tree outside his home in Staten Island's New Dorp Beach neighborhood on Nov. 14. Ingenito decorated the tree with coffee cups and breathing masks. (NY Post: Chad Rachman)

from a fallen spruce in front of his Sandy-ravaged New Dorp home, the commander-in-chief sought out the family and an aide delivered the special gifts.

"It's an honor. It's a once-in-a-lifetime deal," said Joe, who decorated his 7-foot outdoor tree with debris salvaged after the storm.

He was still improvising. The tree outside the home sported a string of white lights, a mask, goggles, a worker's glove, bells, a can of Goofy String, someone's cap and a Hannah Montana bag.

Joe is saving the president's two precious ornaments until 2013, when the family's tree, hopefully, will be back inside.

One depicts a Santa holding a big red bag outside the White House and reads, "I hear there are some kids in the White House this year." The other is a vintage car with a driver and passenger wearing a top hat.

"The ornaments are beautiful, very authentic and detailed," said Debbie, who keeps them in the velvet-lined boxes they came in for fear they would be stolen if they're put on the tree outside.

She can't wait until Christmas 2013, when the family will put them "right at the top" of the tree.

"They will be passed down to the family," said Debbie. "When I go, they will go to my firstborn."

A week after presenting the gifts, Obama gave the Ingenitos a shout-out.

"Today, if you go to Joseph's street, you'll see a lot of damage and debris scattered all over the block," he said.

"But you'll also see the top of that tree, standing tall in front of his house." ∎

Additional reporting by Yoav Gonen and Joe Tacopino

When Joe and Debbie Ingenito celebrate Christmas in their Staten Island home in 2013, their tree will feature this ornament given to Debbie by President Barack Obama. (NY Post: Chad Rachman)

Part 4

MANHATTAN

Left: A view of the turbulent waters in Battery Park on Oct. 31. Above: Cars were submerged as water pumping operations went on through the night in the Financial District on Oct. 30. (N.Y. Post: William C. Lopez)

THE DARK NIGHT

By Chuck Bennett and Jessica Simeone

City's Bright Lights Bow to Sandy

Vast swaths of the city's spectacular skyline went dark on Monday, Oct. 29, as ferocious winds and the sea surge from deadly Hurricane Sandy battered the city.

A quarter-million customers lost power in Manhattan alone.

"Most of Manhattan below 39th Street is out," said Con Ed spokesman Chris Olert, adding that there was no timetable for getting the lights back on.

But the top of the Empire State Building remained lit, glowing amid its darkened neighbors.

Many took to the streets.

"It's not too often you get to see the city dark," said Greg Pearl, 26, an accountant who was taking pictures on the East Side.

A group staying at the Affinia Gardens hotel were told to stay in their rooms. So they bolted en masse to check out the suddenly medieval-looking city.

"We're going to roam the city because I was never in a hurricane before," said Susan Stubel, 42, visiting from Los Angeles.

A deafening "boom" was heard in the East Village near a power facility on the FDR facing the East River — and then the lights went out.

"Con Edison is reporting power outages to a large section of Manhattan stretching from East 39th Street to the lower tip of Manhattan," the utility said in a statement. "The outage was caused by flooding in company substations and engineers are working to correct the problem."

"I haven't seen lower Manhattan shut down before," said Jonathan Lee, 25, who walked across the Williamsburg Bridge with a buddy.

The intersection of Greenwich St. and Murray St. in Manhattan went dark as power went out in much of Manhattan on Oct. 29. (N.Y. Post: William C. Lopez)

"It was scary! I was watching TV, looked outside the window and heard a big explosion and saw a big flash of white light like a firecracker."

–Maritza Mercado

"It's like an apocalypse, like a movie," said his pal, Paul Parhar.

A high-voltage feeder on 14th Street was knocked out, Con Ed confirmed. "When feeders go out they can be real loud," said a utility source.

"It was scary!" said Maritza Mercado, 40, on East 6th Street. "I was watching TV, looked outside the window and heard a big explosion and saw a big flash of white light like a firecracker."

The utility also reported that a storm surge downtown caused a substation equipment failure affecting more than 60,000 customers throughout lower Manhattan and Greenwich Village — including at Con Ed's headquarters.

Some 50,000 New Yorkers were already without power when lower Manhattan went dark.

But it wasn't bad for everyone.

"I think it's fantastic," said Rachel Lindover, 21. "It actually feels like nighttime. For a city that doesn't sleep, it's finally sleeping." ■

Additional reporting by David Seifman, Erin Calabrese and Sally Goldenberg

Left: As power went out in much of Manhattan on Oct. 29, the top of the Empire State Building remained alit. Above: Despite the power outage, the bar at Merchants NY cafe in Chelsea remained open on Oct. 30, lit by candlelight. (N.Y. Post: William C. Lopez)

FLOOD RESCUE ORDEAL

By Rita Delfiner

Citi Security Saves Man, Dog on West Street

Sandy was raging around him as Michael Delacruz left a stalled cab on West Street clutching his dog, Pyapya. A nonswimmer, he was soon up to his neck in floodwater — and was sure he was going to die.

"I thought if I was going to drown, at least he should live," the 5-foot-5 reinsurance underwriter said of the 14-year-old whippet, a cancer-survivor.

"He's like my son. He's gone through so much in his life." Delacruz , 48, yelled for help as he tried to walk and keep both of their heads above the water overflowing onto deserted Hubert Street at around 8 p.m. Oct. 29.

Miraculously, he got an answer — from Rajinda Pal, a Citi security staffer who spotted him as he stood at the Hubert Street loading bay at the north side of 390 Greenwich St., which houses the banking giant's trading operations.

Pal signaled for him to keep going along Hubert Street. Delacruz soon found himself on a submerged elevated sidewalk, where the water level was lowered to his chest.

Balthazar Fortune, a Citi chief security supervisor, and Luis Guzman, a security officer, jumped in the water and pulled Delacruz and Pyapya to safety.

"They just opened their hearts to me," said Delacruz, who noted that the Samaritans, while not needing to swim, still had risked their lives for a stranger. "Those floodwaters, you never know what they're capable of doing."

Seven backup generators at NYU Langone Medical Center failed during the storm surge on Oct. 29, forcing the evacuation of 300 patients. (N.Y. Post: William C. Lopez)

"They just opened their hearts to me. Those floodwaters, you never know what they're capable of doing."

—Michael Delacruz

Delacruz's nightmare began at around 6 p.m., when he decided he and Pyapya — whose name derives from the Hindi word pyaar, meaning love, needed to evacuate the West Street apartment he shares with his partner, Tim Perry, who was at work.

He grabbed a cab, and the driver headed north on West Street.

"I noticed water was seeping into the cab," said Delacruz. As they reached the intersection of West and Hubert streets, the engine stalled, and the water was up to the cab windows. He told the driver he was getting out.

Delacruz said he was thinking of Pyapya.

"I wanted him to live," said Delacruz, who said the dog tried to swim, but he held him close because "I didn't want the waters to sweep him away."

He thinks with sorrow of the victims claimed by Sandy, how "so many from New York and New Jersey lost their lives and homes, and I know I'm very lucky to have met these wonderful people from Citi." ■

rita.delfiner@nypost.com

Opposite: A rescue worker trudges through waist-deep water on Water Street, near the South Street Seaport, as the storm hit on Oct. 29. Above: Patients are evacuated from NYU Langone Medical Center after the hospital lost power. (N.Y. Post: William C. Lopez)

THE FIGHT FOR FOOD
AND TAXICABS
Lower Manhattan Enters Third Day Without Power

By Frank Rosario and Laura Italiano

The candlelit charm is over. Nearly a quarter-million Lower-Manhattanites began a third day with no power on Nov. 1 — another day of vying for cabs, buses and even a loaf of bread.

"This is about money. If you flash cash, you get a cab," James Alamo, 36, said at Essex and Grand streets after the 10th cab passed him by — only to pick up a cash-flashing older guy just up the street from him.

A livery cab driver sped off after Alamo refused his extortionate request for $50 to take him to 34th Street. "They are really gouging us," the hapless traveler said.

"My son is so cold," Michelle Rios, 21, said of her 2-year-old as they waited for the M15 bus at Allen and Grand streets. "I've been waiting here over an hour and a half, and I've seen four buses pass by" — each too full to board, she said.

John Pascale, 56, spent Oct. 31 trying to board a bus out of his blacked-out neighborhood near the state and federal courts in a quest for cellphone reception. "The buses were so crowded, I had to get on the third one that came," he said.

"I got off at 38th Street, and then I had to find a place to charge my phone," he said. A generous pizza proprietor in the East 30s let customers charge their phones, Pascale said. "There were four, five people ahead of me, waiting to use their chargers," he said.

"We have absolutely no bread — not a loaf," said a manager at the Gristedes at South End Avenue in Battery Park City.

"It's strange," noted resident Sergei Artemov, 60, as he waited on a long line there.

"Overnight, things you take for granted, like milk and bread, become hot commodities." ∎

Additional reporting by Amber Sutherland and Rebecca Rosenberg

Cars pack the Manhattan-bound 59th Street Bridge on Oct. 31 as limited mass transit left workers little choice but to drive in. (N.Y. Post: Tamara Beckwith)

CURB
A-PEELED

By Erin Calabrese and Rebecca Harshbarger

Facade is 'Blown Off' in Chelsea

A four-story apartment building in Chelsea partially collapsed on Oct. 29 as winds gusted to more than 50 mph. The front facade on the top floors of the building, on Eighth Avenue near West 15th Street, fell off, completely exposing the rooms inside.

One firefighter suffered minor injuries, the FDNY said.

A tourist staying in the building said she first noticed pieces falling from the ceiling.

"It's an old building. It creaks and things, so initially we didn't think anything was going on," said the tourist, Natasha Stelmaszek, 56, of Seattle.

She went outside to take a look at the building, which has a business on the first floor, and noticed a crack.

"I decided to go upstairs to the fourth floor and then down to the second to let everyone know," she said.

"And as a group, we just figured it was time to get out."

Isabelle Boussard, visiting from France, said she and her family packed their bags and crossed the street.

"Ten minutes later, we watched it fall. It was crazy," she said.

City Council Speaker Christine Quinn surveyed the damage. She told NY1 she was going to check whether it was an illegal hotel.

A call to the Department of Buildings and the building's owner were not immediately returned. ∎

Additional reporting by David Seifman

Firefighters survey the damage on Oct. 29 at a Chelsea apartment building whose facade slid off amid Sandy's high-speed winds. (N.Y. Post: Brian Zak)

HOPEFUL NEWS ON CRANE

West 57th Street Construction Site Stabilized

Residents and businesses were displaced by a broken crane dangling 1,000 feet over West 57th Street. "The crane is currently stable," said Mayor Bloomberg, as residents — briefly allowed back into nearby buildings — were instructed to take essential belongings and return the following week.

The crane's boom was blown back over its engine as the storm grew fierce at about 2:30 p.m. on Oct. 29.

The mayor said city engineers have been in the building since Oct. 30, and have "determined the ties that bind the [crane] tower to the building are secure."

By Nov. 2, he said, workers would be able "to tie the boom to the building."

At that point, officials could reopen West 57th Street — closed since Oct. 29 at the height of the storm — and begin taking down the broken crane at the under-construction luxury building.

Crane-industry consultant Tom Barth said the process could take weeks.

They'll "eventually construct another crane next to it to take down this one," the mayor said. ∎

Sandy's fierce winds on Oct. 29 blew a crane's boom over its engine at a construction site on West 57th street, forcing the evacuation of nearby residents and businesses. (AP Images)

NY SAMARITANS
Selfless Neighbors Help Elderly and Disabled

By Frank Rosario and Kevin Fasick

"I'm still pretty strong for my age," says Jane Rapp, 65.

This is an understatement. In the days following superstorm Sandy, Rapp ferried precious water in heavy buckets from a curbside fire hydrant up to her elderly neighbors in her 21-story building at 75 Montgomery St. on the Lower East Side.

"There are elderly people who are bedridden on the upper floors," she explained. "They're very sick and they need help."

With no electricity and, therefore, no water pump, taps were dry throughout the upper floors of building. It was Rapp who lobbied the city to turn on the hydrant so some water was available, albeit at street level.

After sunset, when the halls are pitch black, Rapp wore a light strapped to her head as she carried her heavy buckets up the stairs, looking something like an urban coal miner.

"I can make fewer trips by bringing up two buckets of water. It's pitch black in the stairwells and at first, it was really frightening going up and down," she said.

"It's been incredibly overwhelming trying to live like this," she said. "But we have to remember the spirit of old NewYork.

"We don't need light and technology to takecare of each other — just some good old-fashioned hard work."

On the Upper East Side, residents of 200 East End Ave. — many of them elderly — found themselves without power after the storm flooded their basement.

And just like that, their neighbors across the street at 180 East End offered to take them in.

That was welcome news for Mike Traub, 74, who suffers from muscular dystrophy and gets around with a scooter — but who lives on the ninth floor of 200 East End, and had no way of getting downstairs.

Or so he thought.

The building's porter, Luis Cortes, carried him down.

"I knocked on the door and said you need to get out but he said he couldn't walk. I said no problem and carried him down nine flights. It was difficult, but I did what I had to do" said Cortes, 53.

Another building employee, José Murillo, carried Traub across the street.

When he got to his host's apartment, "They were very welcoming and food was pushed on us. Cakes, coffee, salads, soups."

Traub's wife, Bonnie, said, "They were super wonderful. New Yorkers are the greatest people in the world."

One of those who played host to displaced neighbors was Robert Horowitz, 82, a part-time Traffic Court judge in Nassau County, and his retired teacher wife, Micki, 81.

"I spoke to my wife and we said [to the people working downstairs] 'Send someone up who needs a bed.'"

They sent up Dorothy Kreindler, 80.

"They were true good Samaritans, as many people were there and at 170 [East End]," Kreindler said. "They are wonderful people." ∎

A volunteer carries water into in New York's Baruch Housing Project on Nov. 2. Volunteers went door to door, distributing food and water to the building's elderly and disabled residents. (Getty Images)

Part 5

NEW JERSEY, LONG ISLAND AND **THE REGION**

Left: Damage to the Liberty Island shuttle dock is seen on Nov. 2. The island, home of the Statue of Liberty, sustained major infrastructure damage. It is scheduled to reopen by July 2013. (N.Y. Post: Chad Rachman) Above: A volunteer helps clean out the Hurricane Sandy-damaged Evangel Revival Community Church in Long Beach, New York, in late November. (N.Y. Post: Charles Wenzelberg)

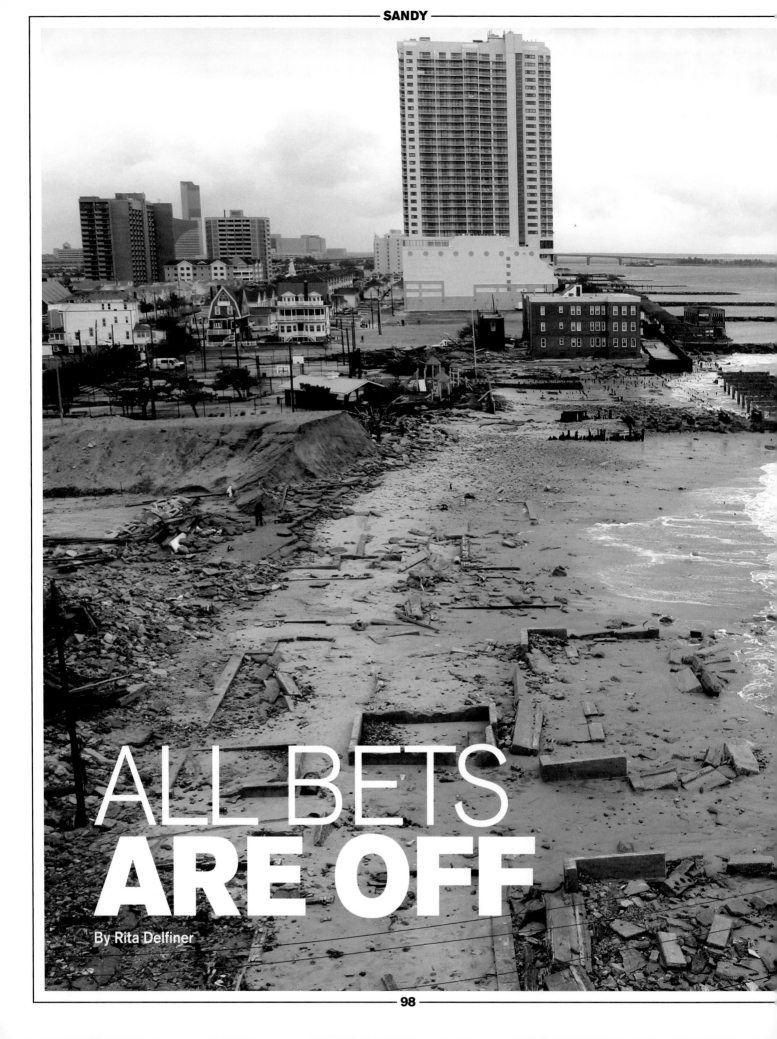

ALL BETS
ARE OFF

By Rita Delfiner

Atlantic City Under Water

Lady Luck was a no-show in Atlantic City. Sandy arrived in full force on Oct. 29, and the hurricane gave the city such a brutal pounding that most of it wound up under water.

"The city's basically flooded," said Willie Glass, Atlantic City's public-safety director.

The city and its 12 casinos were ordered to evacuate a day earlier. Despite plywood over casino windows, some of the neon signs still flashed.

Gov. Chris Christie urged those on the barrier islands who hadn't yet left to get away during low afternoon tide.

"This is not a time to be a showoff, this is not a time to be stupid," he said. "This is the time to save yourself and your family."

And in a poke at Atlantic City Mayor Lorenzo Langford, he said, "For those elected officials who decided to ignore my admonition, this is now your responsibility."

The warnings didn't stop Ron Skinner, a Harrah's employee, from going to the beach. "It is what it is," he said. "I don't worry much."

Still, a 50-foot section of the northern end of the famed Atlantic City Boardwalk was torn away by floodwaters. A 13-foot surge of seawater was reported.

Hurricane Sandy reduced brick buildings and the boardwalk along Atlantic City's coast to foundations and pilings. (AP Images)

Emergency-management officials, aided by National Guard troops, said they were going through the city areas most at risk, looking for people who didn't move from their homes.

Bob McDevitt, president of the main Atlantic City casino workers union, stayed put, but not without reservation.

"I have never seen so much water in the inlet; it's totally underwater," he said. "When I think about how much water is already in the streets, and how much more is going to come with high tide tonight, this is going to be devastating. I think this is going to be a really bad situation tonight."

At one point first responders in Atlantic County and Atlantic City were ordered to return to shelter and cease operations, but later were allowed to venture back to the waterlogged streets. ■

Left: Waves crash against a previously undamaged Atlantic City pier as Sandy arrived on Oct. 29. (Getty Images) Above: An aerial photo taken Oct. 31 shows the devastation the storm left in Atlantic City. (AP Images)

OBAMA HAS WARM HUG FOR JERSEY

President, Gov. Christie Take Helicopter Flight

By Jeane MacIntosh

President Obama on Oct. 31 got a bird's-eye view of the unprecedented devastation unleashed on New Jersey by superstorm Sandy as he took a helicopter tour with Garden State Gov. Chris Christie.

Both men insisted politics played no role in the visit, but the image of Mitt Romney cheerleader Christie — who once called Obama "the most ill-prepared person to assume the presidency" — and the commander-in-chief together presented a powerful political image just six days before the presidential election.

The one-hour flight came as the National Guard continued to rescue stranded residents, while 2 million Jersey residents remained without power and the storm death count in the state rose to eight.

"It's really important to have the president of the United States acknowledge the kind of suffering that's going on here in New Jersey and I appreciate it very much," said Christie, who has heaped praise on Obama in the aftermath of Sandy.

"We're going to work together to make sure we get ourselves through this crisis," he added.

Standing together later in the day, Obama promised that the federal government would "be here for the long haul."

"We will not quit until this is done," he said.

"The directive I have given [is] we are not going to tolerate red tape, we are not going to tolerate bureaucracy."

He said restoring power is "a top priority," adding that he has instituted a "15-minute rule" in which his team has been told to return any state official's call within that time frame.

"If they need something, we figure out a way to say yes," the president said.

During the helicopter tour, Obama saw a decimated Jersey Shore, including the town of Mantoloking, where fires — which destroyed 14 homes just after Sandy hit — were reignited by natural-gas leaks, officials said.

Entire portions of Long Beach Island were underwater or covered in mud and several feet of sand.

Farther north, in Seaside Heights, sand and water filled several blocks, homes were flattened and the popular boardwalk was largely decimated.

"The whole town looks like a beach with houses sprouting from the middle," said a sad resident.

As Christie and Obama concentrated on the shore, the National Guard was in Hoboken, across the Hudson River from Manhattan, rescuing stranded residents in the badly flooded northwest end of the one-mile-square town, which smelled of smoke and fuel.

Nearly a dozen large Guard trucks carried parents, children and pets to higher ground near Hoboken's City Hall.

"They came in and took people out, which was good," said resident Brett Johnson. "There's flooding and mold. It stinks. Food is starting to go bad." ■

Additional reporting by Geoff Earle, Kirstan Conley and Post Wire Services

President Obama in embraces Donna Vanzant in Brigantine, New Jersey, on Oct. 31. Vanzant lost her marina business when Sandy hit. Obama promised significant federal help. (AP Images)

SAD EYESHORE

NJ Evacuees See Wrecked Homes

By Kate Kowsh and Todd Venezia

When Heidi O'Rourke and her husband, Steve, got to see their ruined New Jersey beach home for the first time on Nov. 9, the waves of devastation finally hit them.

"It's a hundred times worse than we were expecting," Steve exclaimed, as he stood near his wrecked house in Holgate on Long Beach Island.

The structure had been ravaged by Superstorm Sandy — flooded, covered in sand and left with massive holes, including one that exposed a bathroom for all to see.

"The force of the water just blew the walls right off," he said. "The whole main floor is destroyed."

Heidi added: "Our refrigerator was in the garage. Now it's five houses down."

The O'Rourkes were among hundreds of Jersey Shore home owners who finally got a chance to see the full measure of Sandy's horror yesterday, as they were given a brief opportunity to visit their damaged houses and grab a few items.

"Everything's wrecked," said Raymond Stone, 62, whose house is a block from the beach in Holgate. "There was so much sand, it was like snow over everything."

Marianne Hurley, 67, who owns Hurley's Inn, a 10-room hotel across from the Holgate beach, said the destruction was "like a nightmare."

"I can't believe this happened," she said. "It's gonna be a long road ahead of us."

In the town of Ocean Beach, about 30 miles north, near Seaside Heights, residents were also allowed a first look at the destruction yesterday.

"That was my home. That was where I live. Or where I lived," said Kathy O'Brien, who burst into tears after finding her house had been inundated. "It's gone now. It's very emotional."

Despite the heartache, many tried to say positive.

"We had a Jacuzzi in the back yard, and we cannot find it," said Vinny Renz, 55, of Holgate. "You have to have a good attitude about it, or it will eat you alive." ■

Residents survey damage to beachfront houses in Long Beach Island, New Jersey, on Oct. 31. (AP Images)

DIG THIS:
I LOST POWER—TWICE

Nor'Easter Impacts
Sandy Victims

By Dana Sauchelli and Dan MacLeod

Some frustrated Long Island residents got their electricity back for a New York minute before the powerful nor'easter cruelly took it away again. Maddie Eliantus, 29, of Elmont, praised her maker when the lights finally came back on after 10 days without juice.

But when she got back from work at around 4 p.m. on Thursday, Nov. 8, she found the power out again.

"It must have been only 10 hours we had power," she said. "I'm upset because I only got it last night, and today, I'm going to be in the cold again.

"I just don't feel like sleeping in the cold anymore. Ten days without heat! It's crazy. I'm frustrated."

A neighbor, Donny Pascal, said he suffered a similar fate. He lost power during Hurricane Sandy and had it restored by the Long Island Power Authority, only to lose it again in the nor'easter.

Some 122,000 Con Ed customers in the city and Westchester were without power early on Nov. 8, with an estimated 55,000 of those customers losing power after the nor'easter dumped as much as 7 inches.

By early this morning, the number of customers without power in the city and Westchester had dropped to about 43,000, Con Ed said.

The storm also knocked out power in 123,000 homes on Long Island.

Sheila Labranche, 40, of Elmont, lost electricity during Sandy and was dark for four days before getting back power. But the lights were knocked out again by the new storm.

Now she's back to boiling water to keep warm.

"I'm freezing. Look at me...It's just so scary because it's so cold," she said.

Adaku Ubanai, 40, also of Elmont was thrilled when the lights came on.

"Oh, my goodness — you should have seen the joy here. The kids were so happy," she said.

But a day later, they were back in the dark.

There were still 39,681 without power in the Rockaways, LIPA said.

Residents blasted the utilities.

"We're getting caught in bureaucracy, and it's a real shame," said Dan Mundy, president of the Broad Channel Civic Association in Queens. ∎

Additional reporting by Erin Calabrese

Donny Pascal, of Elmont, Long Island, digs out on Nov. 8 Mother Nature's latest insult: a half-foot of snow dropped during the nor'easter. The storm knocked out Pascal's power just after it had been restored following Sandy. (AP Images)

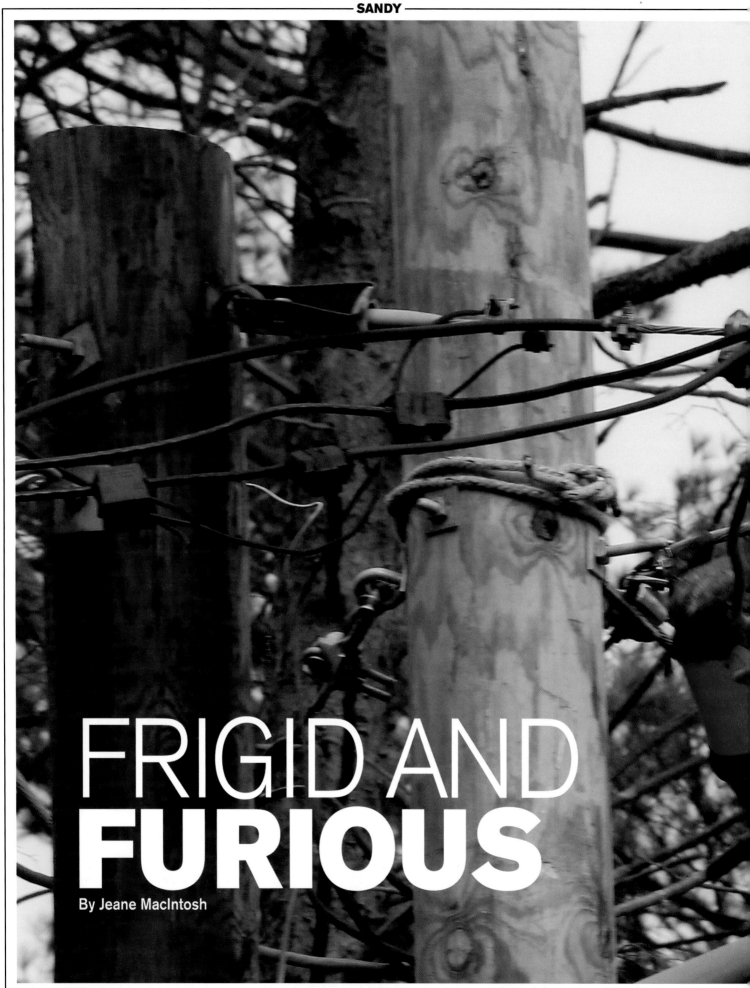

FRIGID AND
FURIOUS

By Jeane MacIntosh

Long Islanders Turn Up Heat on LIPA

Devastated by the double whammy of Sandy and a nor'easter, cold, powerless Long Islanders hit the streets to rail against LIPA as the Nassau County executive said the situation is "beyond urgent."

"We want answers!" residents of Oceanside — which was socked with 6 inches of snow after being ravaged by Sandy's surges — demanded at a rally outside School 8 on Nov. 9.

They booed Rep. Carolyn McCarthy and Hempstead's town supervisor, accusing them of not making enough noise on their behalf.

Despite line crews working round the clock, LIPA hasn't given a timetable for power restoration for the more than 170,000 customers still in the dark.

In Oceanside and nearby Island Park, frozen residents, some now homeless, huddled around garbage-drum fires for warmth and appealed to FEMA for help.

At a press conference with federal, state and local officials, Nassau County Executive Edward Mangano said, "Long Island's power is past the point of crisis...To put it in terms that Washington can readily understand, LIPA's power is at Defcon 2. The condition is beyond urgent."

Private volunteers from all over the country arrived with aid — including doctors from Michigan and Colorado and two paramedics, sent by FEMA from St. Louis, who slept in an ambulance in Oceanside. ∎

An electrical crew member contracted by LIPA works on overhead lines in Melville, New York, on Nov. 19. Power remained out in many parts of Long Island three weeks after Sandy hit. (Getty Images)

STILL THANKFUL

By Kieran Crowley

Long Island Leukemia Kid and Kin Overcome Several Storms

With their Long Island home destroyed by Hurricane Sandy and their income lost, it could be said that the Heckman family had very little to be thankful for on Thanksgiving 2012.

But then there is the persistent good health, against all odds, of the middle child of the Heckman brood, 6-year-old leukemia patient Steven.

That, along with the news that Yankee pitcher Joba Chamberlain will help raise funds for the boy's medical care, means "there's always hope," said mom Danielle, 29.

"It was stupid," Steven said about Sandy, just the latest of the storms he has had to weather.

"It destroyed the house," he said of the family's two-bedroom Cape Cod cottage in Amityville.

"I can't be in because it's bad air. I had a cough, a croupy cough. I want to live in the house. The one thing I miss the most is my bunk bed. We couldn't have Thanksgiving."

Steven takes a daily chemotherapy pill, submits to weekly spinal-fluid testing, and has endured numerous emergency-room visits.

In November, the three Heckman kids — also including Alexandra, 9, and Juliana, 3 — plus Mom and Dad were squeezing into the one-bedroom apartment of friends in Farmingdale.

Dad Steven Sr. gave up his pool-construction company to help care for his son.

"I do believe God is watching over us," said Danielle as she prepared to cook turkey, stuffing and pumpkin pie in their temporary home. ∎

Six-year-old leukemia patient Steven Heckman (far left) of Amityville, New York, took part in a ceremony with New York Yankees first baseman Mark Teixeira at Yankee Stadium on Aug. 4, 2012. Less than three months later, Heckman's family's home was destroyed by Hurricane Sandy. (AP Images)

Part 6

RECOVERING
& GIVING A
HELPING
HAND

Jolly old Kris Kringle arrives with a bag full of toys in storm-demolished Belle Harbor, Queens, bringing smiles to children. (AP Images)

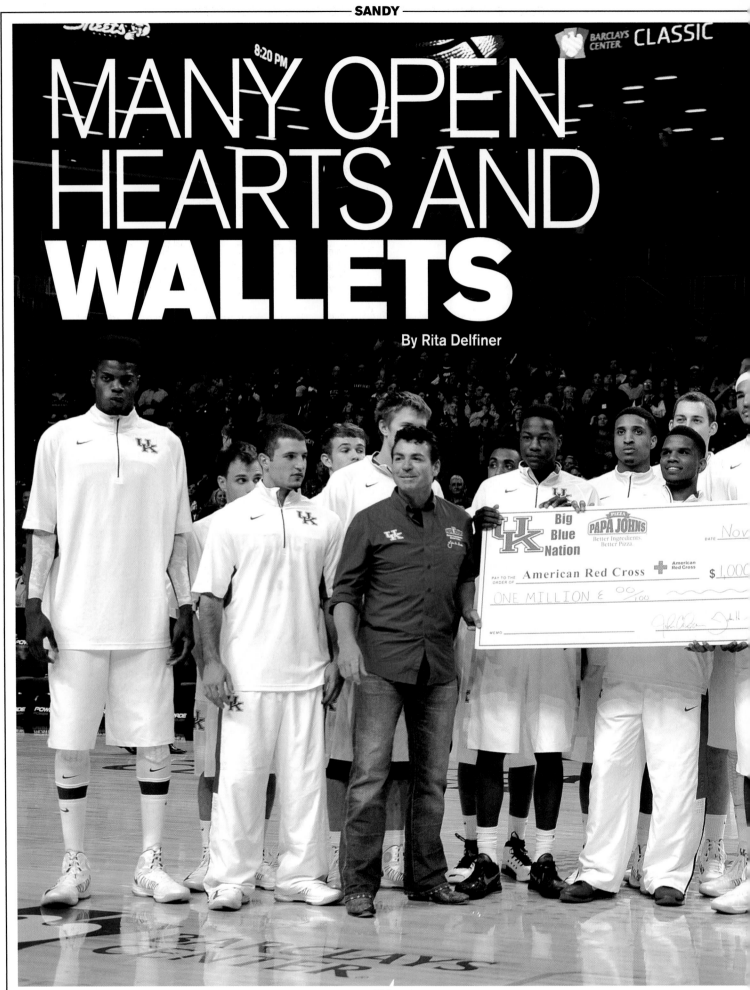

MANY OPEN HEARTS AND WALLETS

By Rita Delfiner

Individuals and Corporations Contribute to Sandy Relief

Helping hands — from individuals to corporations — swiftly reached out with support for victims of Hurricane Sandy, including News Corp., which is donating $1 million.

The company, which owns The New York Post, said it is giving $500,000 to the Mayor's Fund for NYC and $500,000 for relief in New Jersey.

"Our hearts go out to those who have lost loved ones and those families coping with this tremendous natural disaster," said Chairman and CEO Rupert Murdoch and Deputy Chairman, President and Chief Operating Officer Chase Carey.

"But we are also heartened by the stories of communities pulling together, with neighbors helping neighbors through this difficult time," the execs added.

Contributions to the American Red Cross for Sandy storm relief include $500,000 from the Yankees, 50 trucks from Chevrolet and pallets of water from Nestlé Water. The Citi Foundation, which gives the Red Cross an annual $500,000 grant for disaster relief, is donating an additional $1 million.

Red Cross spokeswoman Anne Marie Borrego assured victims that help is on the way.

"We are moving as fast as we can. Road closures have been a challenge, but we will be in the communities we need to be," she said.

Big-hearted New Yorkers pitched in, including 40 students from St. Bonaventure University 70 miles south of Buffalo, headed to the Rockaways with generators, chain saws and pumps.

They're volunteers with BonaResponds, a disaster-relief group formed after Hurricane Katrina by finance professor Jim Mahar. ∎

The University of Kentucky basketball team presents a check to the American Red Cross before their game against the University of Maryland at Brooklyn's Barclay Center on Nov. 9. The Wildcats' Nov. 7 telethon raised $1 million. Papa John's Pizza founder John Schnatter and ESPN analyst Dick Vitale also took part in the presentation. (Getty Images)

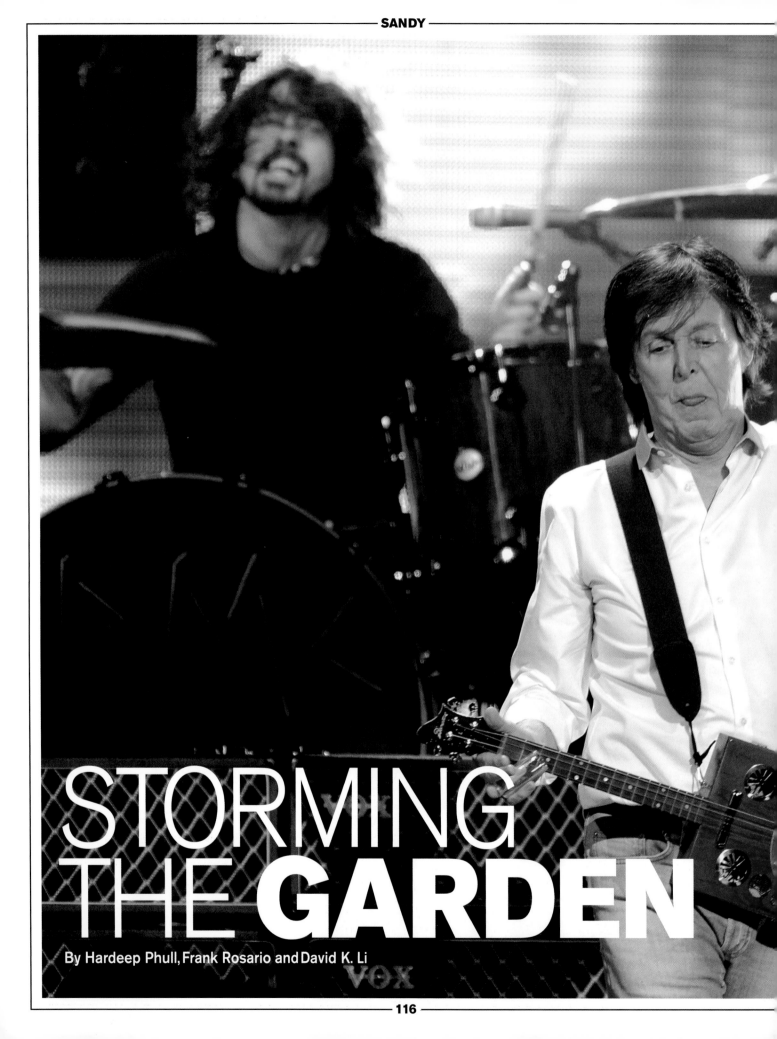

STORMING THE GARDEN

By Hardeep Phull, Frank Rosario and David K. Li

Music Legends Band Together to Raise Over $30M for Sandy Relief

Victims of Hurricane Sandy forgot their problems for six precious hours on Dec. 12, as New Jersey's favorite sons — Bruce Springsteen and Jon Bon Jovi —led a world-class lineup that rocked Madison Square Garden.

A mind-blowing gathering of music all-stars, comics and Hollywood heavyweights took the stage at MSG to raise at least $30 million dollars for hurricane relief. Organizers are hoping to top the $56 million raised by the Concert for New York City for 9/11 victims.

As New York songbird Alicia Keys belted out her hit "Brand New Me," Lana Boychuk — from the hard-hit Staten Island neighborhood of Midland Beach — could barely contain her emotions.

"This concert has brought tears of sadness — and hope that parts of New York and New Jersey can be rebuilt again," said Boychuk, 24.

The evening's raw emotions of sorrow and optimism reminded Rockaway Beach resident Ryan Sirgiovanni, 26, what a small price he paid to Sandy — losing two cars in his flooded garage.

"It was tough, but we consider ourselves lucky," Sirgiovanni said at MSG. "The show's been great.

Sir Paul McCartney fires up the crowd during the 12-12-12: The Concert for Sandy Relief concert at Madison Square Garden on Dec. 12. (Getty Images)

Bruce was the perfect way to start the show. He really kicked off the crowd, and you can tell he really is passionate about the show and the cause."

Springsteen's E Street Band summed up the night in one song, a heart-felt rendition of "City of Ruins" about the fall and rise of his adopted hometown Asbury Park.

The Boss said he's praying for Asbury Park and all Jersey Shore towns rocked by Sandy.

"I had tears in my eyes," said 23-year-old Brooklyn resident Katie Rzevskaya. "He was unreal."

And as if the show — organized by the Robin Hood Foundation — couldn't get any more Jersey, Springsteen brought fellow Garden State rocker Jon Bon Jovi on stage for The Boss' anthem "Born to Run." The two later did Bon Jovi's famed "Who Says You Can't Go Home."

Eleanor Killian, a 24-year-old Manhattan resident who works at a Harlem school, said she was so touched by the struggles of her students that she's been volunteering in the recovery effort in Breezy Point, the Queens waterfront community hammered both by the storm and a devastating fire the night Sandy struck.

"It was the most devastating thing I've ever seen," she said at MSG last night. "I think this concert is a testament to how resilient and tenacious the city is. It really says a lot about the artists who came together — at such short notice, too — and how they were so ready and willing to help out."

Springsteen, Bon Jovi, Keys, Roger Waters, Eddie Vedder, Eric Clapton, The Who, the Rolling Stones, Paul Shaffer, Adam Sandler, Kanye West, Billy Joel, Chris Martin, Michael Stipe, Diana Krall and Paul McCartney all performed. One of Sir Paul's final songs was belted out with surviving Nirvana rockers DaveGrohl, Krist Novoselic and Pat Smear.

The concert ended with first responders on stage with Keys to sing her signature "Empire State of Mind." ∎

Additional reporting by Lia Eustachewich

Billy Joel performs during the Dec. 12 benefit concert at Madison Square Garden, which raised more than $30 million for victims of Hurricane Sandy. (AP Images)

IN DOUGH, YO!

Megastars Raise Millions to Aid Sandy Victims

By Jeane MacIntosh

The money poured in. So many people opened their hearts — and wallets — for the epic 121212 Concert for Sandy Relief that its fundraisers could not immediately quantify just how many dollars were hauled in.

The mega-event, boasting an all-star music lineup, had raked in more than $30 million before the six-hour show even started, and insiders estimated that another $10 million to $20 million flowed in online and through the show's celebrity-manned call center.

But show organizer The Robin Hood Foundation declined to even estimate how much its star-studded extravaganza might bring in for victims of the devastating superstorm that ravaged NewYork and New Jersey.

Patty Smith, spokeswoman for the foundation, said, "We want to make sure we have an accurate number to give out...We want to get the money out the door and do the people who need it as quickly as possible."

All of the money raised goes directly to Sandy relief efforts, with the concert costs picked up by its corporate sponsors, Smith said.

Robin Hood's relief fund has already raised $15.7 million, separate from the concert, that has been distributed in aid, Smith noted.

Before the Dec. 12 Madison Square Garden show opener Bruce Springsteen even took the stage, revenue from tickets, corporate donations and sponsorships topped $30 million.

Donations were still coming in yesterday, and a 121212 online auction — featuring memorabilia from the show — was drawing big-bucks bidding.

A Fender bass guitar — signed by Paul McCartney, Springsteen, Roger Daltrey, Billy Joel, Dave Grohl, Chris Martin, Michael Stipe, Eric Clapton, Jon Bon Jovi and other performers — had reached $38,600 late yesterday.

The concert got plenty of day-after buzz.

Mick Jagger sparked outrage on Twitter after a comment he made during the Rolling Stones' performance. "This has got to be the largest collection of old English musicians ever assembled in Madison Square Garden," Jagger quipped onstage. "But I've got to say, if it rains in London, you've got to come and help us, OK?"

"Wait wait wait...did Mick Jagger say if it rains in London we should help them? Was it raining during WWII?" wrote@dwbohle.

Kurt Cobain's mercurial widow, Courtney Love, took issue with McCartney teaming up with the surviving members of Nirvana to do a new song, "Cut Me Some Slack."

"Look, if John [Lennon] were alive, it would be cool," a cranky Love told TMZ.

Kanye West's bizarre skirt-and-leather leggings outfit took on a life of its own, spawning a Twitter site—@KanyesSkirt—that boasted more than 1,000 followers by the morning following the concert.

"Sorry everybody. This is awkward for me too," @KanyesSkirt tweeted. ■

Jersey rock legends Jon Bon Jovi (left) and Bruce Springsteen shared the Garden stage on Dec. 12. (Getty Images)

TAKE OUR PRESENTS, PLEASE!

New Yorkers Sacrifice to Spread Holiday Cheer to Sandy Victims

By Jane Ridley

The O'Shea kids of Marine Park, Brooklyn, had a big-ticket item on their Christmas list: a $400 iPad Mini. But Mairead, 10; Colin, 9; Eamonn, 8; and 6-year-old Siobhan agreed to give up their wish for the pricey Apple product — and funnel all the money from their Christmas presents to victims of hurricane Sandy instead.

The foursome happily signed up for the Secret Sandy program, a charity founded by NYC residents, which through mid-December had matched 3,200 donors with about 1,800 families in need. They bought a walking toy, a Transformers action figure, the Disney movie "Brave" and an electronic science kit for the kids they were assigned, including a baby and a 6-year-old boy.

"Sitting at the laptop ordering the gifts, there was a lot of excitement," says their mother, Louise Bogue, 42, adding that Siobhan, who has Down syndrome, was the most enthusiastic of the four even though she had set her heart on the iPad Mini to play her computer games.

"I'm really proud of them because they discussed the idea at Thanksgiving and decided it was the right thing to do," says Bogue. "They know they are not for want, while other kids have lost their homes, their clothes, their toys."

The O'Sheas are not alone: Whether foregoing Christmas gifts, providing meals for displaced families or volunteering other services, many New Yorkers gave up Christmas or Hanukkah — and brought some much-needed cheer to their neighbors devastated by the October superstorm, which killed 61 locals, caused an estimated $65 billion in damage and by Christmas left 2,111 New Yorkers in transitional shelters.

Husband-and-wife musicians Christel Rice Astin, 38, and Jarad Astin, 37, and their children, Arden, 12, and 2-year-old Riley, traditionally spend Christmas Eve quietly with relatives at their home.

Except this year, they don't have a home.

They've been subletting an apartment in Crown Heights since losing their place and all their belongings in the Rockaways. To "stay sane," they've immersed themselves in volunteering for the Sandy Relief Kitchen program run in conjunction with Two Boots pizza restaurant and based out of Old First Church in Park Slope.

And, just as they'd been doing every Wednesday, Thursday and Friday in the nearly two months since Sandy struck, the Astins spent Christmas Eve delivering more than 300 donated meals to an action center near their former block on Beach 57th Street.

"It's been traumatic for the whole family, but there is no way we can turn our backs on our community," says Christel. "Our Christmas was never going to be the same anyway, but at least we know our neighbors won't be going hungry."

Meanwhile, 10-year-old Jack Neiberg spent his Hanukkah helping fellow comic book addict, Travis Moore, 20, who lost his treasures in the storm.

The Neibergs, who live in Chelsea, bonded with Moore and his family in November after answering a call for volunteers, and drove to the Rockaways to lend a hand. They made a sudden stop at Beach 68th Street. "We came across this family, clearing

out the contents of their ruined home," says Jack's mother, Jill, whose offer of help was accepted by Travis' father, Tony.

For hours, they dragged dozens of trash bags to the curb, full of ruined books, clothing, electronics — and a once-pristine comics collection, now drenched.

Jack laid the comics out on the sidewalk, ink bleeding from the pages, in an attempt to dry them out. But it was too late. Sifting through the collection, he noticed it contained some of his own favorite titles — "Archie," "Spider-Man" — and he felt compelled to help.

"As we drove home, he shook his head and said: 'Mom, we've got to make sure they get some holiday gifts this year.' It really made an impact on him," says Jill, 42.

That night, the Neibergs shared their experience on Facebook and asked people to donate Home Depot gift cards to the Moores. Through mid-December, through their extensive network of friends, the Neibergs had raised at least $2,000

for the family. Tony, an auto mechanic, was able to buy a boiler and flooring for his gutted home.

Nearly every weekend since they met, the two families have gotten together in the Rockaways to work on the renovation.

"We've been really touched by their kindness," says Tony, 46, fighting back tears. "They are truly amazing people, and we feel blessed that they found us."

Best of all was the gift of comics. More than 150 new and vintage comic books were donated by the Twilight Zone, a store in Maryland owned by Bumper Moyer, a friend of one of the Neibergs' Facebook friends. Jack handed over the present to Travis.

His efforts — along with those of all the families who've given up their own celebrations to help others — represent the real meaning of the season, say locals.

"The message is that in giving, we receive," says Bogue. "That message will last a lot longer than the latest action figure or the new iPad." ■

An artificial Christmas tree known as the "Tree of Hope" stood in an empty grass lot in Union Beach, New Jersey. The tree, which was rescued from a pile of trash and wreckage left by Superstorm Sandy and put up by a local resident in November, was visited and decorated by people who considered it a symbol of hope. (Getty Images)

SANTA BRINGS HO-HO-HO-RICANE **RELIEF**

Brooklyn Hero Leads Massive Toy Drive

By Selim Algar and Dana Sauchelli

Here comes Sandy Claus. A bighearted New York political consultant took off the business suit and put on a beard to hand-deliver toys to kids victimized by Hurricane Sandy.

Michael Sciaraffo, 31, of Brooklyn, spearheaded a toy drive that began with his local Gravesend church and has blossomed into a national movement.

"I was sitting at home watching these terrible scenes from the storm," Sciaraffo told The Post. "Usually, these things are happening far away, in other countries. But this was right here. I had to do something."

To the delight of stunned children, Sciaraffo — in full Kris Kringle regalia — trudges up to their Sandy-ravaged homes with a stuffed sack over his shoulder and rings the bell.

"The faces of these kids when they see me is just wonderful," Sciaraffo said. "There is nothing like it."

His favorite encounter came in the form of one little girl who was fast asleep when he knocked on the door.

"Her mom wanted me to wake her up," he recalled.

"So I sat on her bed and tapped her. She opened her eyes and said, 'Santa, why are you in my dream tonight?'

"I told her that this wasn't a dream, that I was Santa and I had come to give her presents. Her face just lit up."

Through Dec. 21, Sciaraffo planned to light up a total of 113 little faces, and his list was growing.

The phenomenon began when the former Hillary Rodham Clinton presidential campaign aide and state Assembly staffer put up fliers at his local chapel and asked for donations.

When the bins began to fill, he started a Facebook page and took requests from people to deliver to children in need.

In total, a whopping five tons of toys have been gathered thus far.

"I can't deliver all of it," Sciaraffo said. "So, at this point, I'm going to do what I can and have the rest sent. I want to get toys to every child who asks for them."

Sciaraffo's crusade is only one of many Sandy-specific acts of charity taking place this year.

Attorney Joe Mure has turned his Queens home for 19 years into a Christmas-theme wonderland to raise money for victims of diabetes. But this year's bash will benefit kids in need of Sandy relief. ■

Michael Sciaraffo, as Santa Claus, presents a toy to nine-year-old Alex Creamer in the Belle Harbor section of Queens. Using Facebook, Sciaraffo started a charitable enterprise to collect and personally deliver toys to children affected by Sandy. (AP Images)

PICTURE-PERFECT
ENDING

Good Samaritan Restores Staten Island Couple's Photo Album

By Joe Tacopino and Pedro Oliveira Jr.

Sandy washed away their treasured memories — but a wave of kindness brought them back. A Staten Island couple was convinced they had lost a lot more than furniture when the October superstorm ravaged their home — they had to throw out a waterlogged photo album, including family wedding pics from the '50s.

"Everything was floating," said Mary Buongiorno, who lost other photo albums with her husband, Lenny. "We were looking at the pictures — with bacteria and water, you don't know what to do.

"I figured it was gone forever."

Distraught, the couple left the pictures on the lawn of their Midland Beach home to be thrown out.

But good Samaritan Mike Valente, a bus driver, couldn't let the memories go to waste. He found the photos on the side of the road and got to work immediately.

"When the album came to my house, it smelled terrible," said Valente, of Eltingville. "It was sitting underwater for two weeks, the leather and cardboard absorbed the water and there was also

sewage there."

He worked for five weeks to restore the album, chipping away at it a few hours each night to clean, dry, rescan and restore the photos on his computer.

Mary was at a friend's house last week when Valente showed up with the surprise.

"I never expected anything," she said. "When I opened it up, the pictures were just overwhelming!"

Valente had a simple explanation for his random act of kindness.

"We have traditions and we have things that we do in my family; I'm all about memories," he said.

Brooklyn photographer Rob Loud knows the story too well.

"Several people close to me lost homes, cars, countless possessions," said Loud, 33, who lived in Long Beach for four years and moved to Clinton Hill in May. "Everyone always says, 'If there's one possession you cannot get back, it's photos.'"

So the shutterbug last week volunteered his time and talents to host a photo shoot with Sandy victims who lost their family portraits — and help them regain some of the memories lost during the storm. ∎

On Nov. 6, recovery workers in Staten Island found these water-logged photos from Rosalind Silletto's aunt's wedding party 43 years earlier. Many Sandy victims reported losing similar family treasures to the storm. (Getty Images)

Built in 1855 and once known as the Princess Cottage, this home on Front Street in Union Beach, New Jersey, stood for more than 150 years before it was torn in half by superstorm Sandy. (Getty Images)